Cindi Johnson

P9-DOH-084

The
Power *of* Our
Words

Teacher Language That Helps

Children Learn

Paula Denton, EdD

NORTHEAST FOUNDATION FOR CHILDREN

The stories in this book are all based on real events in the classroom. However, in order to respect the privacy of students, names and many identifying characteristics of students and situations have been changed.

© 2007 by Northeast Foundation for Children, Inc.

All rights reserved. No part of this book may be reproduced in any form or by any electronic or mechanical means, including information storage and retrieval systems, without permission in writing from the publisher, except by a reviewer, who may quote brief passages in a review.

ISBN: 978-1-892989-18-5
Library of Congress Control Number: 2006938201

Cover and book design by Helen Merena
Cover and interior photographs © Peter Wrenn. All rights reserved.

Thanks to the teachers and students of Six to Six Interdistrict Magnet School, Bridgeport, Connecticut; Kensington Avenue School, Springfield, Massachusetts; Community Preparatory School, Providence, Rhode Island; K.T. Murphy School, Stamford, Connecticut; B. F. Brown School, Fitchburg, Massachusetts; Hart Magnet Elementary, Stamford, Connecticut; Washington School, West Haven, Connecticut; and Reingold Elementary School, Fitchburg, Massachusetts, who welcomed Northeast Foundation for Children to take photos in their classrooms.

Northeast Foundation for Children, Inc.
85 Avenue A, Suite 204
P.O. Box 718
Turners Falls, MA 01376-0718

800-360-6332
www.responsiveclassroom.org

14 13 12 11   10 9 8 7

Printed on recycled paper.

ACKNOWLEDGMENTS

This book took about a year for me to write, but it represents knowledge gained over many years of learning about the power of our words to influence perceptions and behavior. Many people helped me learn along the way.

I would like to thank RUTH CHARNEY first of all. This book builds directly on her thinking about teacher language as she shared it in *Teaching Children to Care* and many speeches and workshops over the years. It was in that book that the categories of reinforcing, reminding, and redirecting language in the *Responsive Classroom* approach were first articulated. I have been fortunate to have Ruth as a model, mentor, and supportive colleague for the past twenty years.

In addition, I would like to thank other colleagues from the Greenfield Center School who were extremely influential in shaping my understanding of the importance of listening carefully to children; speaking clearly, succinctly, and respectfully; stressing the deed, not the doer; and tying our words directly to actions:

> CHIP WOOD'S booming yet calm redirection to his class—"Middles, freeze!"—could be heard rolling through the halls of our little school from time to time. Chip's characteristically gentle and reflective tone made such redirections all the more powerful.

> JAY LORD gained the willing cooperation of adolescents with his positive outlook. His playful yet firm and respectful words supported his students to fill their classroom with the excitement that comes from problem solving and creativity.

> MARLYNN CLAYTON engaged five- and six-year-olds' best thinking by asking deceptively simple sounding but highly skillful questions that conveyed genuine interest in and respect for their ideas.

> ROXANN KRIETE demonstrated the power of using precise language and building vocabulary in order to empower children to learn and grow. She shared with her students a love of words.

I have been privileged to observe and work with many teachers, too numerous to name, over the last ten years in public schools throughout the country. All of them have added to my knowledge of the ways teacher language can help children learn. Each of them has helped me to develop my thinking for this book.

Everyone at Northeast Foundation for Children gave of their support and comradeship throughout this project. Many of you talked with me about the ideas in this book as I struggled to clarify and articulate my thinking. Thanks to ROXANN KRIETE for chats over coffee; to MARY BETH FORTON for conversations both scheduled and unscheduled; to ELIZABETH NASH, who read, listened, and helped me fill in gaps; and to LYNN BECHTEL, who was always ready to listen when I dropped by.

ALICE YANG was a very special editor. She admired and encouraged, listened and questioned, and added significantly to the thinking and organization of this book. Alice made it all come together in a way that conveys my message more effectively than I ever could have done without her.

Colleagues who shared feedback on my drafts were also enormously helpful in the development of this book. They include RUTH CHARNEY, PAMELA PORTER, MARLYNN CLAYTON, SUZY STARK, LESLIE ALEXANDER, ROXANN KRIETE, and MARY BETH FORTON.

JANICE GADAIRE FLEURIEL proofread the manuscript with care and efficiency. I appreciate her eye for detail.

HELEN MERENA, graphic designer, made the book shine. From selecting the cover photo to choosing the font and type size, she brought to this work her characteristic artistry and commitment to quality.

Finally, I would like to acknowledge the work of other authors who have guided me to increase my skill with language as a professional teaching tool. They include, among others, RUDOLF DREIKURS, ADELE FABER and ELAINE MAZLISH, JIM FAY and DAVID FUNK, ROBERT GARMSTON, PETER H. JOHNSTON, ALFIE KOHN, JANE NELSEN, and BRUCE WELLMAN.

For my mother and father, Tommy and BeeGee Robinson,
who first taught me to be careful what I say, and to my husband,
Steven, and sons, Christopher and Lakota, who continue
to be my best reasons for doing so.

CONTENTS

Introduction

Language is one of the most powerful tools available to teachers. It permeates every aspect of teaching and learning. We cannot give a lesson, welcome a child into the room, or handle a classroom conflict without using words. Children cannot do a science observation or reading assignment or learn a classroom routine without listening to and interpreting their teacher's words. And what they hear and interpret—the message they get from their teacher—has a huge impact on how they think and act, and ultimately how they learn.

Consider this scene: Lunch is over and the children, returning noisily to their classroom, are slow to settle into their seats. Some chatter loudly while others rummage through their belongings or lean across desks to get in on some action across the table. Calmly, Ms. Gibbs rings a chime, a well-rehearsed signal for the children to be quiet and attend to her words. She waits a moment until the last child is settled, quiet, and looking at her, then says in a conversational voice, "I see that everyone is ready for math. Let's get started." The children's focus shifts to math, and the lesson gets under way.

A few simple words, carefully chosen and said with the appropriate tone and pacing, transformed the atmosphere and led the children to a mental place where they could learn at their best.

Here's how a different teacher might have handled the scene: Raising her voice to be heard above the chatter, the teacher nearly shouts, "Okay, settle down, everyone! Social time is over. We have to get to work on math now."

Although both teachers are responding to the same situation and both want to prepare the children for math, their uses of language send very different messages to the students. In the second example, the teacher's language implies that learning is about resisting pleasurable natural inclinations such as talking to friends so that we can do the less pleasant "work" of learning math. The phrase "have to" further reinforces the idea that math is something unpleasant that the children would not choose to do on their own. And by raising her voice to get the children's attention, the teacher conveys that she gains control by overpowering them.

Contrast this to Ms. Gibbs's language, which implies that learning is about working together to achieve mutually desirable and pleasurable goals. Attention is gained not through an overpowering voice, but a soft chime. Early in the year, Ms. Gibbs had carefully taught the children what the chime meant—stop whatever you're doing and pay attention to the teacher—and had given the children opportunities to practice responding to it. With that grounding, the use of the chime now allows the teacher to send a signal without having to overpower the children. She can then talk in a tone and volume that is in keeping with theirs. Her language implies that, given the opportunity, the children can and will draw upon their own skills and intrinsic motivation to prepare to learn. In particular, the teacher reaffirmed this expectation when she said that the children were "ready for math."

The power of language makes language a prime teaching tool. As teachers, we come into the profession because of our belief in education and our desire to nurture children's growth. Language helps us do this nurturing. By learning to use teacher language to its full potential, we can more effectively turn our visions for students' learning into reality.

In this book, the term "teacher language" refers to the professional use of words, phrases, tone, and pace to enable students to engage in active, interested learning and develop positive behaviors. This kind of language rests on a deep and abiding faith in the goodness in children, a belief in their desire and ability to learn. It also rests on faith in teachers' ability to teach, to bring out the best in children. The book will discuss which kinds of language support these goals and beliefs and why. It'll offer practical guidelines and concrete examples of language to adopt as well as language to avoid.

First, a closer look at how language affects children's growth.

THE POWER OF LANGUAGE

Language is far more than the simple expression of thoughts, feelings, and experiences. As psychologist Lev Vygotsky said, language actually shapes thoughts, feelings, and experiences. It produces "fundamentally new forms of behavior." (Vygotsky 1978, 24) Language does this in several ways: It molds our sense of who we are; helps us understand how we think, work, and play; and influences the nature of our relationships.

LANGUAGE MOLDS OUR SENSE OF WHO WE ARE

Our words can shape identities. What we say to others can deeply affect their sense of who they are and who they might become. The words of a teacher may have special power in this regard. I was struck by this fact when my friend Don told a story about his experience with singing as a child. When Don was five, his mother, who loved to sing, enrolled him in a children's choir. "I had a very deep, booming voice for a little boy and, I suppose, a tin ear as well," Don recalled. "But I loved going to choir practice and singing with the other kids. I liked to stand in the front row and sing my heart out!" One day, as the group was preparing to perform, the music teacher said to Don, "Let's have you move to the back row and try just mouthing the words." "That was the moment I learned that I was not a singer," Don said, chuckling. "I never wanted to go back to choir practice again."

This music teacher was probably trying to be gentle with Don, and Don now tells this story with laughter. But the teacher's belief that he was not a singer, and never would be, came through to him loud and clear, even at the young age of five. The fact that Don, now forty-eight, still remembers and tells this story shows that the teacher's words had a deep impact on his developing sense of self. The words narrowed Don's sense of possible identities rather than broadening them. They conveyed a belief that his ability to sing was not only poor, but also would never change. Rather than trying to teach him how to sing better, this teacher effectively put a stop to Don's motivation to learn to sing.

What might this teacher have said instead? Perhaps "Don, you really put your heart and soul into singing! Would you like to learn more about it? I have some ideas." These words would have opened the doors to learning for Don and supported his budding identity as one who loves to sing. They would have conveyed the belief that the ability to sing can be developed in those who want to learn. Although Don may never have become a professional singer, he might very well have learned satisfying ways to contribute to the choir and continued to enjoy singing into adulthood.

LANGUAGE HELPS US UNDERSTAND HOW WE THINK, WORK, AND PLAY

In addition to shaping our sense of who we are, words help us understand how we think, work, and play. I experienced this recently in my own work as a graduate student. During a discussion with one of my professors about a field project I was doing, I shared some problems and my approach to solving them. The professor listened, then said, "You seem to take a very intuitive approach to teaching." Though I had been a teacher for twenty years and had plenty of time to reflect on my teaching style, I had never thought of myself as intuitive. I wasn't even sure what it meant to teach intuitively. But my interest was piqued and the word "intuitive" resonated in my mind as I continued to go about my work. I began to notice the times I responded to students in ways that worked and seemed to arise spontaneously. I began to see aspects of my practice that I'd been unaware of and to understand these as "intuitive" teaching.

This new consciousness would have been powerful by itself. But in my case there was a second benefit: When I became curious about where this intuition came from, I became more aware of the amount of time I spent informally reflecting on my teaching. I realized that the more time I spent reflecting, the more often I used effective teaching practices that appeared spontaneous and intuitive. I learned that what was truly valuable in teaching was not so much spontaneity and intuitiveness, but effectiveness. I saw that the appearance of spontaneity and intuitiveness was a byproduct of repeated doing, reflecting, adjusting, doing again, reflecting, and so on. All this learning was sparked by my professor describing my work as "intuitive."

Teachers can use language to expand children's perceptions and insights just as my professor did for me. "I notice lots of juicy adjectives in your story," we might say. "I really get a sense of how your character looks and feels." Naming or describing a specific attribute— the use of juicy adjectives—alerts the writer to an important element of her writing and how it impacts the reader. Alternatively, a teacher might say only "You're a good writer" or "Great work!" Although such words may help the child form a positive identity, they don't help her understand what makes her a good writer. She doesn't hear words that help her see the elements that make her writing effective. Without seeing, she has a harder time knowing what to do similarly next time or what strengths to build upon.

LANGUAGE INFLUENCES THE NATURE OF OUR RELATIONSHIPS

Our words and tone of voice play a critical role in establishing the nature of our relationships. As teachers, we can choose language that forges a relationship of trust or one of mistrust between us and our students. I once had a student who had a reputation as one of the scariest bullies in the school. He was used to relationships with adults and other children that were built on threats and punishments. My tendency was to threaten and punish him as well. "Jim, if you don't stop it, no more recess! You're scaring the other children."

One day when I took him aside to deal with yet another incident, I was inspired to try some of the new conflict resolution language that I had been learning. "Jim, I saw you pushing Adam and Silas. You were yelling, too. Can you help me understand what happened from your point of view?"

Jim stared at me for a moment. Then his face, tense with anger, began slowly to relax. "You want me to tell you about it?" he asked hesitantly.

"Yeah. I want to help, and I can only help if I understand how things are for you," I assured him. Jim slowly began to explain his point of view. He didn't stop being a bully at that moment—or that year—but we began to build a relationship based on more trust of each other. As a result, Jim slowly became less defensive and more open to my attempts to help him stop the bullying.

A teacher's words may also shape students' relationships with each other and with their learning. We can create an atmosphere of curiosity, engagement, and respectful interactions. "Listen carefully and see how many good questions your classmates come up with to ask at the museum." "Look at all the different patterns people in this class made with the blocks." "How many details can you detect in this set of minerals?" "Who heard an idea from someone else that they'd like to try?" "How will you help each other do your best learning today?" "How can we take care of each other when we go out to play kickball?" "What would you like to learn about Native Americans?" These are all questions and statements that influence children to respect and value their peers, and to become curious and engaged learners. Our careful choice of words and tone leads children to build positive relationships with their learning and with fellow learners.

THE GOALS OF TEACHER LANGUAGE

Skillful teacher language is language that supports students in three broad ways: developing self-control, building their sense of community, and gaining academic skills and knowledge. Across all of these areas, language is a tool that helps teachers articulate a vision, convey faith that students can attain it, give feedback that names students' strengths, and offer guidance that extends students' skills.

DEVELOPING SELF-CONTROL

It's safe to say that all teachers want their students to learn self-control. The key word here is "learn." We're not born with self-control; we learn it as we grow. There are critical conditions that facilitate this learning. As psychologist Edward Deci explains, to develop self-control, children have to have a growing sense of autonomy and competence—a sense that they are controlled by themselves rather than by a force from outside, and a sense that they are capable of achieving desired outcomes. (Deci and Flaste 1995) Our job as teachers is to help children develop this sense of autonomy and competence. We do this by giving them opportunities to become aware of themselves—what they do well, what they're interested in, how they're feeling, how they're changing—for children need to have this self-awareness in order to make conscious choices about their behavior. We also do it by giving them opportunities to practice generating ideas, making decisions, following through, and reflecting on the results.

Language plays a huge role in this equation. We can use words that reveal specific positive behaviors and skills we noticed, or words that offer only unrevealing generalities. We can use a tone of voice that encourages children to practice the skills that lead to autonomy and competence, or a tone that does the opposite. Effective language can be quite simple: We might say "I see you're working hard to add details" in a warm, calm voice. To a child who struggles with doing thorough work, this may be enough to provide motivation. To a child who is impulsively flicking paper at classmates during quiet work time, we can say firmly yet kindly, "What should you be doing right now?" or "Show me how you will follow our rules for quiet work time." When a child begins to act out because he doesn't know how to solve a math problem, we might say calmly, "What's a way we talked about for handling frustration if you don't get something right away?" These simple reminders help students develop and reinforce a repertoire of constructive behaviors. They show faith in students and prompt them to draw upon their own resources to remember behavioral expectations and act on them. In this way, they help students experience autonomy and competence and develop self-control.

BUILDING A SENSE OF COMMUNITY

In addition to a sense of autonomy and competence, we all have a basic human need to feel a sense of belonging. (Deci and Flaste 1995) For children in a classroom, this feeling is critical if they are to be motivated from within to learn. When they feel safe and valued, they're more willing to do the risk-taking and the cooperative give-and-take that lead to greater learning. (Jensen 1998)

We can foster all students' sense of belonging by using language that encourages everyone to value and practice cooperation, respect, and empathy. Following a science activity, a teacher says cheerfully but without gushing, "I noticed cleanup went quickly today because you were all helping each other." This gives children feedback about aspects of their behavior that were helpful. After observing hurtful behavior during recess, a teacher convenes a class meeting. He introduces the purpose of the meeting, then, using a matter-of-fact voice, poses an open-ended question to the whole group: "How might it feel to be told 'no' when you ask to join a game?" This encourages the children to imagine feelings they have not yet felt or to share feelings they have felt. With such language, teachers can guide students to behave in ways that allow all classmates to participate fully in classroom life and to see all classmates as members of their community.

GAINING ACADEMIC SKILLS AND KNOWLEDGE

Most of the language we use professionally is aimed at helping students develop academic skills and increase their knowledge. "I wonder how many different things we can observe about this bird's nest" fosters in children the skill of careful observation and the attitude of curiosity. "What are you most proud of about your work?" encourages reflection and self-critique. "It seems like you're using context clues to figure that word out" helps the child become conscious of a useful strategy that she might use again in the future.

Our language can also help children learn from each other, and here's where a sense of community again comes into play. When children feel safe with each other, they can engage in ways that stretch their academic skills and knowledge. Vygotsky calls this reaching into their "zone of proximal development," or that space between what they can do on their own and what they can do with help from someone a step or two more skilled. (Vygotsky 1986/1934) For example, a child who can't read a book on her own might be able to read it with a class-mate who's at a higher reading level. The classmate might supply words the child doesn't know or take turns reading paragraphs with her. The two might discuss their ideas and questions about the book. All this pulls the less skilled child toward more complex reading and deepens the other child's skills as well. But in order for this kind of deep, con-structive engagement to happen, students need to trust and respect each other, and a teacher's language is vital in helping the class build that trust and respect.

Finally, a byproduct of a teacher's skillful use of language is that the students often begin using language more skillfully themselves. For example, if in giving feedback on students' work, a teacher routinely names specific positives she notices (for example, by saying "You used a metaphor that makes the reader think") rather than issuing a global praise (such as "Good job!"), students may soon adopt that way of speaking when giving feedback to each other. (See Chapter 5 for more on this kind of reinforcing language.) And when the teacher models good listening by using pauses and paraphrasing, children are likely to learn to do the same. (See Chapter 4 for more on skillful listen-ing.) The result is that the classroom becomes a richer place of coopera-tive learning, with children more actively helping each other grow.

THE PROCESS OF CHANGING OUR LANGUAGE

Learning to use teacher language to its full positive potential means becoming aware of our habitual ways of speaking and the messages, positive or negative, that these may be sending to students. It means stepping back to "hear" ourselves and reflect, "What do I say? What tone do I use?" We can then try on and practice new words, phrases, tones, and pacings to replace any ineffective language patterns we may be using. Appendix B describes a language change process and offers tips that can help along the way.

This process of language change can feel different to different people. For some, a new way of speaking comes relatively quickly. For others, it's a slower evolution. Some teachers say that using new teacher lan-guage feels awkward or "phony" and "contrived" at first. Be assured that it just feels that way because we're not used to it. If our intention behind the words is positive—if we truly believe in students' desire and ability to learn and to behave in helpful ways—our communica-tion will feel sincere to them, even if it isn't technically polished or if it still sounds foreign to us.

For some teachers, perhaps especially those who've been teaching for a while, the awkwardness may be particularly unsettling because we're dealing with teaching, our field of expertise—an area of life that we're knowledgeable about, precisely the area in which we're not sup-posed to be awkward. This is an understandable reaction. It can help to remember that feeling unsettled or awkward is often a necessary and natural stage in learning and will pass with practice.

Whether language change comes quickly or slowly, the prize is a more satisfying way to teach. Our classrooms become places where children learn to take care of themselves, their learning, each other, and the world in a different, more joyful way. In short, better language makes us better teachers and our students better learners.

WORKS CITED

Deci, Edward L. and Richard Flaste. 1995. *Why We Do What We Do: Understanding Self-Motivation*. New York: Penguin Books.

Jensen, Eric. 1998. *Teaching with the Brain in Mind*. Alexandria, VA: Association for Supervision and Curriculum Development.

Vygotsky, Lev. 1978. *Mind in Society*. Cambridge, MA: Harvard University Press.

CHAPTER ONE

General Guidelines for Teacher Language

During the course of any school day, teachers can easily find themselves needing to speak with students in a dozen different ways, depending on the situation. This book will go into many of those situations and ways of speaking. First, this chapter will discuss five general guidelines for the use of teacher language. These underpin all the specific strategies offered in the rest of this book. The guidelines are:

1. Be direct and authentic.

2. Convey faith in children's abilities and intentions.

3. Focus on action.

4. Keep it brief.

5. Know when to be silent.

While these principles may seem simple, it's in reflecting on the details embedded in them that we truly come to understand their power.

BE DIRECT AND AUTHENTIC

When our language is direct and authentic, when we say what we mean and mean what we say, children learn that they can trust us. They learn that we won't use language to trick, manipulate, or confuse them. This feeling of safety must be in place if children are to take the risks that are necessary to learning—to try out fledgling skills, to explore their own and others' thoughts, and to take on challenges. Moreover, direct and authentic teacher language simply allows children to feel respected and to know clearly what the teacher means.

SAY WHAT WE MEAN: USING DIRECT LANGUAGE

Many of us learned to use indirect language as a way to gain easy, cheerful compliance from children. For example, as a new teacher, I found I could often get children to do what I wanted by pointing out what I liked about other children's behavior. "I like the way May and Justine are paying attention," I would cheerfully announce while impatiently eyeing Dave and Marta fooling around in the corner.

When this strategy worked, it was because the children wanted to mimic the desired behavior so that they, too, would win praise and recognition from me. My language did nothing to help them develop autonomy or self-control. And it didn't even always get the children to behave as I wanted them to. I remember well one particular day. It was time to begin Morning Meeting, time for the children to finish their arrival routines and come sit in a circle in the meeting area. This was a well-rehearsed routine. I gave the signal to come to Morning Meeting, but most of the class continued to wander around, chatting and ignoring the signal.

"I like the way Henry and Lucien are sitting on the rug," I said loudly to the rowdy and inattentive group. As they had been doing more and more the past few days, the class ignored me. And why shouldn't they? If I liked the way Henry and Lucien were sitting, that was nice for the three of us, but it had no bearing on the rest of the class, which had much more compelling things to do at that moment than please me.

My clever strategy was useless. What I should have done instead was speak directly. I should have first used a signal to gain the students' attention, and then told them firmly and calmly, "Come to the meeting rug and take a seat now."

Another language pattern that many teachers use to soften commands in hopes of making them more palatable to children is to phrase directions as questions. "Could you all go back to your seats now?" we find ourselves asking, when what we mean is "Everyone go back to your seats now."

"Everyone go back to your seats now" may seem less respectful than the less direct "Could you all go back to your seats now?" In reality, it's the indirect language that is disrespectful of students despite our best intentions. When I said "I like the way Henry and Lucien are sitting on the rug," I was trying to manipulate the other children to do what I wanted without them being conscious of my control over them. This is also true of directions phrased as questions. It's more respectful simply to tell children what I want them to do because it is honest.

It's true that many children who hear "Could you all go back to your seats now?" will know that it means they are to go back to their seats. But some children, whether it's because they're less verbally skilled or too distracted at the moment to pick up on subtleties, may truly believe they have a choice—to go back to their seat or not—and that both choices are acceptable. They may feel confused or duped when they choose not to go back, only to have their teacher respond with anger or impatience. By contrast, "Everyone go back to your seats now" tells the children that yes, they have two choices—to go back or not go back—but one of the choices is not acceptable. If they still choose not to go back, they do so knowing it's an act of defiance.

CHOOSE AN APPROPRIATE TONE OF VOICE

Our tone conveys an enormous amount about how we're feeling and what we're truly thinking, perhaps even more than our actual words. It can override the overt meaning of our words and sour our communication in an instant. For example, the simple reminder "What should you be doing right now?" asked in an even, matter-of-fact tone is respectful and achieves the intended purpose of enabling students to keep themselves on track. But the same words in an angry voice become an attack; said with a sigh, they convey lack of confidence that the student will ever do the right thing.

Sometimes teachers twist their tone on purpose. Consider the phrase "Excuse me." "Excuse me" said in a warm, matter-of-fact tone means that we want forgiveness for our mistake. But the same words said with emphasis on the second syllable of "excuse" ("Excuse me!") or with a stridently questioning tone ("Excuse me???") become "You're being rude," "You're being stupid," or "You're being sassy." Using a singsong voice and drawing out the syllables ("Exxxx-cuuussse meeee") means "I'm reminding you to mind your manners."

What happens when we use these raised, fake questioning, or singsong tones? Our communication becomes indirect and unauthentic. My experience is that regardless of our intentions, the result is that children tend to feel humiliated and resentful, or at least confused. They may stop trusting their teacher and stop trusting the classroom to be a safe place.

In general, a warm, matter-of-fact tone is what teachers should aim for. It conveys authenticity, respect, and directness. If what we want to do is remind students to use their manners, we should do that directly—for example, by asking in a straightforward tone, "What did we say about disagreeing respectfully?" And if we want to draw a student's attention to rude behavior, we could issue, in a firm and kind voice, a redirection such as "Robbie, friendly words." (See Chapters 6 and 7 for more on reminders and redirections.)

Be careful of sarcasm slipping in

As many teachers know, it can be easy for sarcasm to slip into our classroom language, especially after a long day. Sometimes we insert sarcasm thinking it will provide some comic relief; other times we're just tired and it slips in without our even knowing it.

While sarcasm may have a place in literature, comedy, and other arenas, it can be damaging in the classroom, where the teacher's role is not to entertain or be buddies with the children, but to maintain a professional teacher–student relationship. Direct and authentic language is a tool of this professionalism, and sarcasm is the antithesis, since the intended meaning in sarcasm is the exact opposite of the words used. It is also most commonly used to insult. The American Heritage® Dictionary (Pickett 2000) defines sarcasm as "a cutting, often ironic remark intended to wound" and "intended to make its victim the butt of contempt or ridicule."

Superficially, sarcastic comments may add a bit of humor to an otherwise tense situation. "John, what part of 'Put your phone away' don't you understand?" a teacher may say, mimicking a line from pop culture. The children laugh, and the teacher thinks she has shown that she is hip and has a sense of humor. But John has just been embarrassed, and his trust in his teacher diminishes. The position of the teacher may be diminished in the other students' eyes as well, even if they laughed, because they no longer see the teacher as an authority that protects their emotional safety but someone who freely uses the currency of insult.

For younger elementary school children, the use of sarcasm may also be confusing. They may sense from their teacher's body language that they have been insulted or that something is funny, but they may not yet comprehend the concept of irony and may not "get" the intended message. If comic relief is what is needed, it's better to take a break from the normal routine and play a tension-relieving game or two. Alternatively, we can simply repeat our directions or give a direct reminder and be ready to follow through with actions if students do not respond appropriately.

MEAN WHAT WE SAY: FOLLOWING THROUGH ON OUR WORDS

Just as important as saying what we mean is meaning what we say. When children know that teachers will follow through on their words, they're likely to take the words seriously. If I tell my class that they must speak softly, using "inside voices," then it's important that I hold to this expectation. Suppose I'm working with a small group, and the rest of the class is getting louder and louder. It may be tempting to keep going and stop the class only when they're so noisy that I can't hear the students I'm working with. But that would tell the class they don't have to take my words seriously. What I should do is take action as soon as I hear the first voice rise above the acceptable level. I could use a signal for attention and then issue a reminder about inside voices, or I could direct the noisy student to move to a spot closer to me.

Meaning what we say implies we should say only what we can, and will, follow through on. If I know I'll allow loud talking because I won't feel it's truly a problem, then I should reconsider telling the children they have to use soft voices in the first place. My words carry the most weight when the students see that I back them up with action.

AVOID OVER-GENERALIZATIONS

Over-generalizations are common in teacher language. "This is going to be hard," we might say at the beginning of a new unit or new activity. Our intention may be to show empathy or to alert students to gear up for extra effort, but what we've done is presented a sweeping statement as being true for everyone when it may not be. In fact we don't know that the new unit or activity will be hard for everyone. What about the students who don't find it hard? What's the message to them? "This is going to be hard" may also cause some children to feel the task is hard when they wouldn't have found it particularly difficult otherwise. Similar problems result when a teacher tells a class "This will be easy" or "This is going to be fun."

It's more authentic and supportive to speak with the first-person voice or the tentative third-person voice in these cases. For example, we could say "I found this fun" or "Some people may find this fun." Introducing a challenging book, a teacher could try "It took me a while to get into this book. I'll be interested to hear how it goes for you."

BE AWARE OF THE SIGNALS YOUR BODY SENDS

Body language—our gestures, body postures, and facial expressions— is an important part of authentic communication. Various authorities report that approximately ninety percent of the total impact of a personal communication comes from body language. (Garrison 1984) Much has been written on how to use body language effectively so that it's consistent with what we want to communicate. While this book will not go into this, it's important to point out that when our words are not true to our intentions, our body language is likely to give us away.

For example, a teacher may tell a student that she's ready to listen to him while looking at another group of students. Her words say she's ready to listen, but her eyes tell a different story. "We're having a good day!" a teacher may announce with a steely tone and down-turned mouth. Or a teacher may say, "Let's all just calm down" in a high-pitched voice while wringing her hands.

Students can see such discrepancies. Human brains are very good at monitoring subtleties of facial expressions to read a person's mood and attitude. We do this so rapidly that we often aren't aware we're doing it. This process begins in infancy. (Johnson 2004) Certainly by the time children are in school, they're quite adept at it. And when children see a mismatch between a teacher's words and body language, they may lose trust in the teacher or simply get confused: "My teacher says she's ready to listen, but she doesn't look like it. Should I talk or not?" "The teacher is saying we're having a good day, but he looks like he's mad at us. What does he really think?"

So, what are we to do about these potential discrepancies in words and body language? I believe the most important thing is to be aware of the signals our body is sending, and then use that awareness to check the authenticity of our words. So often, we say things out of habit without quite realizing that our words aren't genuine. If, however, a teacher does a quick body check before saying, for example, "We're having a good day," he may notice his down-turned mouth or hard gaze. This would tell the teacher that the words about to be uttered are not genuine. The teacher then would have two choices: tell the class "We're having a hard day" if it would be constructive to do so, or wait until he's genuinely feeling good about the day before saying "We're having a good day." Either way, the message would be authentic, the students would understand the teacher's message clearly, and they would feel respected.

CONVEY FAITH IN CHILDREN'S ABILITIES AND INTENTIONS

Because language is such a powerful shaper of identity and perceptions, it's vital that teachers carefully use it to open, rather than close, the doors of possibility for children. Our language conveys our assumptions and expectations, which, in turn, influence students' assumptions and expectations. Suppose a teacher says "When everyone is ready, I'll show how to plant the seeds" or "You can look at the chart to remind yourself of our ideas for good story writing." These words convey a belief that children want to cooperate, listen, and do good work, while also giving the children information about how they can follow through on those good intentions.

"Show me how you will follow the rules in the hall" conveys an expectation that students know how to follow the rules they practiced and will do so. "I'll be watching for interesting strategies you discover to help you solve the math problems" conveys both the belief that students are capable of thinking creatively and independently and the assumption that their work will be interesting.

TAKE TIME TO NOTICE THE POSITIVES

Often, showing faith in children's abilities and intentions means taking the time to notice and comment on the things they do well. "You finished cleanup in less than five minutes today!" "You're trying lots of different ideas for solving that problem. That takes persistence." "I see that you're using your dictionary skills." Such observations tell children why we have confidence in them and provide hard evidence that they should believe in themselves. When children believe in themselves, they are more likely to work hard at learning and to enjoy the process.

AVOID BABY TALK

Adults often use baby talk when speaking to infants. We pitch our voices higher and sometimes louder than normal, use a singsong and exaggeratedly cheerful tone, answer our own questions, and repeat a lot. Sometimes we also purposely mispronounce words to sound more like a young child or use the "royal we" (as in "How are we feeling today?"). We may introduce a more breathy quality to our voices and exaggerate syllables in ways we don't when speaking to peers.

While aspects of baby talk do serve important purposes when communicating with babies and pets (Baron 1989), it can be counterproductive when used with school-age children. Baby talk may imply affection, but because it's affection that assumes the listener has limited capacities, it can leave children feeling that we don't take them seriously. It's better to communicate with students in the same voice we would use with adults and to express our caring in straightforward ways. For example, instead of "How are we feeling today?" we can simply say "How are you feeling today?"

BE AWARE OF LANGUAGE PATTERNS THAT TREAT BOYS AND GIRLS DIFFERENTLY

Teachers by and large are very committed to providing equal opportunities to girls and boys, and may be dismayed to discover that unconscious language patterns can often undermine their efforts. Yet researchers have found that from kindergarten through graduate school, teachers are more likely to use supportive language with male than female students. (Little 2004)

Perhaps it's because we've internalized communication patterns from our own schooling or from our larger society, but teachers as a group tend to provide longer wait time for boys, give more eye contact when speaking with or listening to boys, call on boys more often than girls, and say the student's name more often when speaking with boys. We're also more likely to give boys feedback on the quality of their ideas (such as "You've put a lot of thought into that") and to support boys' autonomy by helping them figure things out (for example, "Where could you look to find the answer?" rather than supplying them with the answer). All this is true, according to researchers, regardless of the teacher's gender or ethnicity or the grade they teach.

Because differences in how we communicate with girls and boys are often unconscious, the critical first step is to carefully listen to ourselves to see if we are using language unequally. Are we giving girls the answers right away more often? Do we give boys more wait time? Are we calling on boys more often? As we become more aware of any unequal uses of language, we can make a conscious effort to correct any imbalances.

Often the best way to raise our awareness is to ask a colleague to observe our teaching for an hour or two and take notes about our interactions with girls and boys. Specifically, we can ask the observer to take detailed notes about wait time, eye contact, whom we call on, and what kind of feedback we give to girls versus boys and then to discuss this with us afterwards. Another possibility is to ask someone to videotape us and then evaluate the tape ourselves. It's amazing what can become obvious when we see ourselves on camera.

Focus on Action

Focusing our language on action means connecting abstract terms with concrete behaviors and describing children's behaviors instead of their character or feelings. This kind of language allows children to learn at their best and be their best selves because it tells them how.

Connect abstract terms with concrete behaviors

Elementary school children learn best through concrete activities and interactions with their environment. Teachers, therefore, can communicate most effectively with children by naming specific and concrete actions rather than abstract terms. For example, rather than telling children, "Be responsible," a teacher might try telling them specifically what she expects them to do. "When you come in to class in the morning, first put your things away, and then read the morning message. After that you may talk quietly with classmates." And instead of saying students' behavior is "disrespectful," it may be more productive to say "Remember—kind words and a friendly face."

Sometimes, rather than naming the concrete behaviors ourselves, it's effective to prompt students to do it. For example, to a student who tends to be unfocused during writing time, I might say "What will help you think of good ideas for your story and concentrate on writing them down today?" The student might then respond, "I can look at our ideas chart," "I can find a quiet place to write away from my friends," or "I can tell myself not to stop until I write down three good ideas."

This is not to say that there is no place for the use of abstract terms such as "responsible" and "respectful." It just means that children need plenty of opportunities to associate them with concrete actions. Indeed, many teachers find it effective to articulate with students such classroom rules as "Treat each other with respect" and "Be responsible." These expectations will be most meaningful to children if we help them picture and practice what the expectations look like in different situations, since we can't assume that children already know. When first introducing these expectations and in periodic refresher conversations, we might ask, "What does it look like when people are being respectful of each other when lining up?" and then "What does it sound like?" "If you're being responsible in the cafeteria, what are you doing? What might you be saying?" "What would you be doing to be successful workers during science?" A conversation prompts children's active thinking and allows the teacher to supply ideas if the children are truly stumped. (For more on this topic, see Brady et al. 2003.)

Some teachers make T-charts to help with such discussions. Heading the chart is an abstract term such as "cooperation." Underneath, there's a column of students' ideas about what cooperation looks like—concrete behaviors such as sharing materials or considering everyone's suggestions in a discussion. Next to this column are students' ideas about what cooperation sounds like—perhaps phrases such as "Please," "Thank you," "Can I help?" and "What's your idea?" (See example on next page.)

DESCRIBE BEHAVIOR, NOT CHARACTER OR ATTITUDE

When teachers notice a behavior that they want a student to change, it's more effective to name the desired behavior than say something about the child's character or attitude. I have found myself saying in frustration to a child who chronically does poor work, "I don't think you even care!" While this may allow me to vent, it does nothing to help the child change. It gives the student no feedback about what he or she is doing wrong or right, and it closes down constructive discus-

Cooperation

Looks like:	Sounds like:
Share materials	"Please"
Consider everyone's suggestions	"What's your idea?"
Offer help	"Can I help?"
Take turns	"Thank you"
Ask questions	"Does that make sense to you?"
Listen	"So what you're saying is …?"
Go along when it's not your first choice	"This game isn't my first choice, but I'll play it."

sion and reflection. The child's energy is likely to go toward defending against the negative judgment, not toward examining and changing his or her behavior. Worse, this kind of language can lead the child to accept the judgment and believe that he or she indeed doesn't care.

It's more helpful to issue a positive challenge to this child, such as "Today, let's see if you can think of a way to get yourself excited about this project. What would help you do that?" When we describe desired behaviors like this, the focus is on what students can do. It shows them how they can be their best selves rather than limiting them to a teacher's judgments of their character.

When we must describe unwanted behavior to get students to understand what it is they are to change, it's important to name specific behaviors in a straightforward, matter-of-fact way and to steer clear of making global judgments. Ms. Tobias, a fourth grade teacher, complained to me about a student, Jared, who seldom put effort into his work. She had adapted assignments to try to make them more interesting to him, she had cajoled, and she had set firm limits, such as "You may not go to recess until you do your assignment." Nothing seemed to work. On a particularly trying day, Ms. Tobias hit her limit. "You've got to stop being so lazy," she warned Jared, "or you'll never get anywhere in this world."

I asked Ms. Tobias what Jared was doing that made her believe he was lazy. "Well," she said, "he just sits through lessons fooling with things in his desk. He wanders around the room when he's supposed to be working on independent assignments, and he only does about half the work he's supposed to."

"Try telling him that," I suggested, "without using terms like 'lazy.' And try to describe some things that he does well, too." Together, Ms. Tobias and I rehearsed some specific language that she might use.

Back in the classroom soon after, Ms. Tobias sat down with Jared and described some of his more positive behaviors. "Jared, you're a friendly guy, and I've noticed that kids like to be around you." Then she described the behaviors that concerned her. "I've also been noticing that you often play with things in your desk when it's time to listen to me or to other kids. I've noticed that you wander around the room a lot instead of doing your work and you're only finishing about half your assignments."

"Oh," Jared said. After thinking a moment, he added, "I guess so, but it's hard to concentrate."

Jared and Ms. Tobias began to engage in a conversation about what he could do differently so he could get more work done and how she might help with that. His behavior didn't change overnight, but it did begin to improve slowly as he and his teacher experimented with those ideas.

The shift toward constructive problem solving happened only after Ms. Tobias dropped her use of the term "lazy" and focused on describing the behaviors that concerned her.

KEEP THE WORDING NONJUDGMENTAL

Often our words contain assumptions and judgments that are indirectly stated. This is called "presupposition" because the speaker is supposing something is true but is not directly stating it. An example is "If you really cared, you'd study harder." The indirectly stated assumption is "You don't care." Although these words seem to be about the student's behavior of not studying very hard, it's really about the student's character of not caring.

One problem with presuppositions is that they present an assumption that's not up for discussion. When a teacher says "If you really cared, …," the student isn't given a chance to offer another view of the situation. Naturally the student might become defensive. "I do care!" the student might retort. Now the conversation takes on an adversarial tone, with the student fighting to defend his character and the teacher perhaps feeling compelled to hold ground as well.

A more effective way for this teacher to discuss concerns about studying would be to stick to describing the problematic behavior. An example is "I notice you haven't turned in your homework for several days in a row." This nonjudgmental wording allows the student to offer her take on the situation and for the teacher and student to go into a problem solving mode.

Other examples of presupposition are "Why don't you ever … ?" (as in "Why don't you ever listen?") and "Why do you always … ?" (as in "Why do you always try to outsmart the rules?") These are not genuine questions, but rather accusations. Such messages can undermine a teacher's relationships with students and make it less likely that students will change and grow.

KEEP IT BRIEF

Children need us to speak with brevity. It's hard for them to follow long strings of words. I sometimes wonder if this is why they say they got "yelled at" when I gave them what I thought was a "firm explanation." Even though my voice isn't raised at all and I am in fact being quite reasonable and calm, the children hear only an overwhelming jumble of words, perhaps along with body language that says they're being corrected for some misbehavior. This basically feels to them like they're being yelled at.

Long explanations, however reasoned and well-intentioned, are usually counterproductive. "When you go out to recess today, be sure to remember to follow the rules for using the equipment, because yesterday some kids got hurt and I'm pretty sure it was because they weren't following the rules. You were doing really well for a while there, but lately it seems like you're getting kind of careless, and that's got to change or we may have to use recess time to review and practice the rules. I know you don't want that, so let's have a good recess today."

By the time the teacher is finished talking, many of the students will be thinking about other things. Few will have followed the entire explanation.

Children often actually understand more when we speak less. Instead of the above explanation, a teacher might say, "Who can tell us the rules for using equipment at recess?" This gives children an opportunity to remind themselves of the rules. Another approach might be to say, "I'll be waiting to hear about the ways in which you made recess safe for everybody today." If the expectations for recess have been adequately taught and practiced, children will be able to understand and make use of such a reminder. Not only would additional explanations be largely lost on them, but after a long string of words, the core message to play safely would likely be lost as well.

LEAVE OUT THE WARNINGS

It can be tempting to warn children what will happen if they don't heed reminders and directions. For example, if a class is playing danger-ously at recess, it might seem natural in the moment to say to them, "If this kind of playing continues, we may have to use recess time to review and practice the rules." But bear in mind that such warnings are gener-ally not effective and too often come across like threats.

The problem with threats is that they convey three negative mes-sages: First, they tell children that we think they're unlikely to behave well. Second, they emphasize the teacher's power to get children in trouble rather than the children's power to take care of themselves. And third, it makes the fixing of our mistakes (in this example, the reviewing and practicing of recess rules) feel like a punishment and therefore some-thing to avoid, rather than a positive way to learn and grow. Children get these messages loud and clear. Warnings or threats thus undermine both children's self-confidence and their trust in the teacher. If a teacher believes the class needs to review and practice recess rules, it's better simply to have them do this than to hold it out as a threat.

KNOW WHEN TO BE SILENT

The skillful use of silence can be just as powerful as the skillful use of language. Silence allows for children's voices. It provides time for thinking, rehearsing what to say, and sometimes for gathering the courage to speak at all. To be sure, our days are often so tightly scheduled and fast paced that allowing time for silence may seem difficult, if not wasteful. But silence is essential to the optimal development of self-control, community, and academic knowledge. And teachers who have allowed silence usually find that it doesn't take as long as they thought. Little bits of silence go a long way.

Below are four examples of the skillful use of silence in the classroom.

PROVIDE WAIT TIME

Researchers tell us that when teachers wait three to five seconds before they take responses to a question, more students respond, and their ideas are more thoughtful and complete. This wait time seems to allow students to do higher level thinking. (Rowe 1974; Swift and Gooding 1983; Tobin 1980) Most teachers wait much less than three to five seconds, though: Typically they wait only one second to call on students after asking a question. (Rowe 1974) Yet few among us, child or adult, can form a complete thought in this amount of time. In the rush to have an answer—any answer—we shortcut or skip the thinking and go straight to talking. We come out with answers of questionable quality, shortchanging our learning as a result. By simply pausing a few seconds to call on students, teachers can raise the quality of classroom conversations.

Teacher modeling is critical here. If we want students to pause and think before speaking, we should do the same ourselves. After a student makes a comment, we can wait a few seconds before we make a comment. Our pace sets a pace for the entire classroom. If we take our time responding, students are likely to do the same—plus our comments are likely to be more thoughtful. Moreover, by pausing a bit before responding to students, we're showing respect for them. We're saying "I want to make sure you've had a chance to express your idea completely and accurately before we move on" and "I want to think well about what you said before I respond."

Many teachers report that pausing three to five seconds can feel uncomfortably long at first. The key is to stick to it, perhaps counting silently to mark the seconds. With practice, this pace will begin to feel more natural and will eventually become automatic.

To make wait time more successful, we can teach children to wait for a signal from us before raising their hands to respond to a question. This allows all the children time to think without a sea of waving hands distracting them or causing them to feel like failures if they don't also have an immediate response. Without waving hands, the wait time is also less likely to feel long. Rather than a forced silence threatening to burst, the seconds become a calm space for thoughtful reflection.

Related to providing wait time is slowing down our words. We need to speak more slowly with children than with colleagues and friends. One four-year study of 10,000 children found that a slower pace of talking combined with steady eye contact improved literacy and reduced behavior problems. In the words of researcher Ken Rowe, "Teachers speak far too quickly. There is too much information going through the [students'] auditory gate. Either nothing goes through or what goes through is garbled." (Doherty 2004) Simply slowing down our words allows children time to process and make meaning of them.

LISTEN TO WHAT STUDENTS HAVE TO SAY

Sometimes teachers simply talk too much. In our eagerness to guide and inform, we fill the air with our pearls of wisdom when we should be asking our students for their pearls, then listening carefully to what they have to say. Not only does listening to students model respectful interaction in a community of learners, but it actually helps students learn because speaking is an important means of formulating knowledge. Children are more likely to learn and remember the content they have spoken about.

For many of us, skillful listening takes some practice. It means resisting the impulse to finish thoughts for children when they articulate slowly or fumble for words. It means that we don't interrupt to correct, elaborate on, or repeat their words, or even to affirm or praise what they're saying. To listen is to hold our silence while maintaining eye contact until the speaker is clearly done and to try to understand what the speaker is saying before formulating a response. This means that we pause before we reply. It may mean we paraphrase the speaker's message before adding our own thoughts or moving to another speaker or topic. (See Chapter 4 for more about pausing and paraphrasing.)

REFRAIN FROM REPEATING DIRECTIONS

An important way of using silence is to resist the impulse to repeat directions. If I want students to take their homework as part of their dismissal routine and we've practiced that routine well, I should give that direction once, check to see if there are any questions, and stop. I should resist reminding them one last time to get their homework as they gather their things and line up for dismissal. This helps children develop autonomy because it gives them a chance to remember the direction themselves and experience the consequences of either remembering or forgetting. If I'm too diligent with constant reminders, the children are less likely to learn to take responsibility themselves.

This does not mean, of course, that I let the children flounder if they have trouble remembering the direction or are confused by it. But there's a difference between helping them figure it out and repeating the direction. Instead of immediately repeating the direction, it can be valuable to try the "helping" step. For example, if I tell the children to gather their art supplies before getting into their groups, and right away everyone gets into their groups empty-handed, chattering and laughing, it would be appropriate for me to say, "Freeze! What should you be doing right now?" If I notice an individual child having trouble with a direction I gave, I might ask, "Would you like some ideas?" or even wait until the child asks for advice before I say anything at all. In all these cases, the children are given a chance to remember and to figure something out for themselves.

RESIST THE TEMPTATION TO USE VOICE-OVERS

A voice-over is a repeating of a student's response right after it's uttered. For instance, I ask the class, "How many days are in a year?" A student responds, "365," and I quickly repeat, "Right, 365," before going to my next question. Or I ask, "What kind of a person do you think Johnny Appleseed was?" I call on Amos, who says, "Kind," and I say, "Kind. What else?" Kate says, "Strong to plant so many trees." I say, "Okay, strong. Who has another idea?"

When I am tempted to use voice-overs, it's because I want to affirm students' words and make sure everyone has heard them. The unintended message, however, is that the children's words are important only if I repeat them, and that the rest of the group needs only to listen to me, since I'll always repeat anything I deem important.

When I catch myself using voice-overs, I try to remember the power of silence. By not repeating, I allow the student's voice to stand on its own, establishing for the whole class that it's important to listen to each other. If classmates couldn't hear what was said, I ask the student to repeat it in a louder and clearer voice. This is more affirming of students' words than echoing them.

SUMMARY

The general guidelines outlined in this chapter serve as the foundation for effective teacher language. The following chapters will look at various types of teacher language in depth and give recommendations for specific situations. All those further ideas and strategies have, as common threads running through them, the five principles described in this chapter:

* Be direct and authentic.
* Convey faith in children's abilities and intentions.
* Focus on action.
* Keep it brief.
* Know when to be silent.

Incorporating these principles into our daily communications with students is critical to building a classroom where students feel safe, respected, appreciated, and interested in learning. The power of teacher language cannot be overstated. The language we use with students every day influences how they see themselves, their teacher, their classmates, and their experience with learning. By paying attention to this power and using it to open rather than close the doors of possibility for children, we help them become self-confident, engaged learners.

WORKS CITED

Baron, N. S. 1989. "The Uses of Baby Talk." *ERIC Digest*. Eric Document Reproduction Service #ED 318230.

Brady, Kathryn, Mary Beth Forton, Deborah Porter, and Chip Wood. 2003. *Rules in School*. Turners Falls, MA: Northeast Foundation for Children, Inc.

Doherty, Linda. 2004. "Children Drowning in a Sea of Blah." *The Age* (November 1). www.theage.com.au/articles/2004/10/29/1099028 201302.html.

Garrison, L. 1984. "Communicating the Nonverbal Way." *Journal of Business Education* 59(5): 190–192.

Johnson, Steven. 2004. *Mind Wide Open*. New York: Scribner.

Little, Deandra. 2004. "Gender Dynamics in the Classroom" in *Teaching a Diverse Student Body: Practical Strategies for Enhancing Our Students' Learning*. 2nd ed. University of Virginia Teaching Resource Center. http://trc.virginia.edu/Publications/Diversity/PDFs/TOC.pdf

Pickett, Joseph P., editor, et al. 2000. *American Heritage® Dictionary of the English Language*. 4th ed. Boston: Houghton Mifflin.

Rowe, M. B. 1974. "Wait-Time and Rewards as Instructional Variables, Their Influence on Language, Logic, and Fate Control. I. Wait-Time." *Journal of Research in Science Teaching* 11: 81–94.

Swift, J. N. and T. Gooding. 1983. "Interaction of wait time feedback and questioning instruction on middle school science teaching." *Journal of Research in Science Teaching*, 20(8): 721–730.

Tobin, K. G. 1980. "The effect of an extended teacher wait-time on science achievement." *Journal of Research in Science Teaching* 17: 469–475.

CHAPTER TWO

Envisioning: Language
as a Spyglass

The beautiful picture book *The Spyglass: A Story of Faith* (Evans 2000) tells of a poor kingdom of barren fields, broken-down homes, and ragged clothes. Here the people were also poor in spirit. They were full of complaints and general grumpiness. One day an old man traveling through this country asked its king for a place to stay the night. In exchange, he would show the king why the kingdom was in such bad condition. The king agreed. When it was time for the traveler to leave, he took the king to a high balcony in his run-down castle and handed him a spyglass.

> *The king looked out through the glass. He could see great
> farms and gardens, magnificent castles and cathedrals ....*

*where there had been barren pasture there were now
fields of grain stretching as far as the eye could see. His
own people were in the fields, their wagons overflowing
with their harvest ....*

*But when the king put down the glass his kingdom
looked the same as before.*

"Nothing has changed."

*"No," said the old man. "Change requires work. But
one must first see before doing."*

*The king again raised the glass. "What greatness this
kingdom holds."*

*"You have seen what might be," said the old man.
"Now go and make it so." (p. 14)*

Just as the old man used a magical spyglass to help the king envision
the possibilities for greatness within his kingdom, teachers can use language to help students imagine themselves behaving and achieving in
ways beyond their current reality. Helping students form and own a
vision of themselves achieving success is a fundamental job of teachers,
and language is a key tool for doing this.

This envisioning is so important because for children as well as adults,
success doesn't always come easily. As the old man said, "Change requires
work." To be inspired to do the hard work, children need a clear and
engaging picture of what is possible, a new and exciting picture of themselves.

For example, a fourth grade class is about to start their research projects. The teacher says, "We've been sharing with each other what animals we like, sports we play, and our other interests. I expect all of you
will choose something you're interested in and do such great research
on it that you become the class expert on your topic. You'll be able to
answer questions about your topic or have a good idea how to find the
answer."

In another class, students are preparing for an upcoming concert. During the arduous rehearsal weeks leading up to the show, they're losing patience and civility with each other. Their teacher, knowing they need a lift, engages them in a discussion of why they're giving the concert. By the end of a fruitful discussion, the students had named several positive reasons. The teacher summarizes their points with an inspiring vision statement: "The most important reason we're doing this is to have fun. When we sing and clap in a happy way, and when we let each other sing and clap in their happy way, we'll all have fun—and look like stars to boot!"

In both examples, the teacher uses language to help children to see— to have an exciting picture in their minds of themselves being something bigger, better, and brighter. When children truly see, they act.

VISIONS ARISE FROM OUR DEEPEST IDEALS

These visions that teachers articulate or help students articulate— visions that motivate children to reach beyond business as usual for something grander—where do they come from? How do we know what will excite our students? In the midst of the daily demands of classroom life, where do we teachers turn for inspiration to create uplifting visions?

The answer lies in reflecting on what is most important to the children. Like adults, children are most motivated by what they care deeply about as human beings, not standards or expectations set by others. The things children spend the most time thinking about, the things that bring a spark to their eyes and a quickening in their speech—these are the rich waters from which to draw effective vision statements.

For most children, "having fun," "being friends," and "feeling happy" rank high among their deeply held values. Other important desires include "feeling welcomed," "feeling safe," "learning a lot," "feeling helpful and needed," "being really interested," "feeling important," "knowing we can work hard and accomplish hard things," and "being able to share our good ideas." These are the kinds of words children use to describe their fundamental human need for belonging, significance, and engagement. (Adler 1958; Deci and Flaste 1995; Dreikurs, Grunwald, and Pepper 1998) Effective vision statements connect the work of school with these compelling personal motivations.

For example, a teacher knows that her fifth graders take great pleasure and pride in learning factual information. So, when talking with them about expected behavior on a trip to Plimoth Plantation, she says, "I expect that each of you, as an explorer of Plimoth, will walk slowly and observe carefully until you find at least one aspect of the village that you really want to know more about." Another teacher, articulating a vision for the year on the first day of school, tells the class, "I expect that in our class everyone will feel welcomed and safe so we can all do our best learning." The teacher who talked to his fourth graders about research earlier in the chapter tapped into the students' interest in their own hobbies and their desire to be "experts." And the teacher preparing the class for the concert connected the upcoming show with the children's desire to have fun and to shine in front of their peers.

Sometimes it's children's complaints that reveal what they most value. As Kegan and Lahey point out in their book *How the Way We Talk Can Change the Way We Work*, it is often our complaints and struggles that reflect our most genuine, deeply held ideals and convictions. The fact that I struggle to hold my temper when I'm feeling mistreated, for example, tells me that I highly value mutually respectful interactions among people. Though I don't always live up to it myself, my ideal is a world in which all people are treated with respect regardless of circumstances. When I find myself complaining about mistreatment of myself or others, I remember that my complaints arise from this value. Naming the positive value allows me to refocus on what I can do to make this ideal happen rather than blame others for my discomfort.

The same applies when we work with children. When students fly off the handle when there's cheating in a game, that's a signal that they value being trustworthy and respecting the rules. If a child gets angry with an assignment that's going poorly, it could be because feeling competent is so important to her. If a student gets grumpy and threatens sabotage when left out of a project, it may be because feeling like he belongs and contributes is a strong need. By being alert to the possible deep needs behind students' upset, teachers can frame motivating vision statements that get students unstuck and on a path toward success.

Notice that none of the examples of vision statements in this chapter are about getting good grades, moving up a level in reading, learning math facts, or being able to name the parts of an insect. Visions are most powerful when they go beyond such realms to express how schoolwork relates to children's larger world. As I write this in the first decade of the twenty-first century, U.S. educational policy is heavily focused on standardized testing and creating pressure among teachers to teach to the test. Yet it's important to remember that being successful in school for its own sake is a limited goal. The most vivid aspects of many children's lives are lived outside the boundaries of textbooks, school assignments, and grades. For these children, school accomplishments by themselves may be uninspiring and meaningless. These goals become important only when they're connected to the children's larger human aspirations, such as feeling engaged and passionate about something, feeling competent and autonomous, and making important contributions to a community they care about.

When to Use Envisioning Language

There are two ways to use envisioning language in teaching: to set a positive tone for future work and to engage children in problem solving.

Setting a positive tone for future work

Because envisioning language is a powerful way to foster student investment and collaboration, this way of speaking is useful when introducing children to new undertakings, from broad ones such as having a successful school year to narrow ones such as having a productive writing period in the next thirty minutes. Using envisioning language to launch new efforts lets children know that we believe in them, while setting an expectation that class members will show empathy for each other and enjoy their shared work. For example:

* As a teacher begins teaching science for the year, she says, "Good morning, scientists! I'm looking forward this year to helping you discover answers to some of the mysteries about the way our world works."

* Ms. Marks, a reading teacher, gathers a group of first graders for their first day of reading instruction. "I'm so excited to be your reading teacher this year," she beams. "My hope is that by the end of this year you will all be book lovers! I hope each of you discovers at least one book that you love so much, sometimes you'd rather read it than watch TV!"

* At the beginning of the year, a second grade teacher wants to set a tone of respectful and collaborative learning for the year. She says, "This year I hope our classroom will be a safe and caring place to learn and that everyone will be able to do their best work." A fifth grade teacher does the same by saying, "This year I hope that students will be friendly with everyone, work hard, and have fun."

* To set clear, engaging guidelines for a writing activity, a teacher says, "Good writers write about what they're interested in and know well. I'm looking forward to learning more about what is important to you as you write today."

ENGAGING CHILDREN IN PROBLEM SOLVING

Teachers can also use envisioning language to help children solve day-to-day problems. One year I taught a class that loved to play Capture the Flag. I observed, however, that the children were spending a great deal of time arguing over who would play the position of flag guard. They were so caught up in squabbling that they had forgotten why they were playing the game in the first place.

To remind them, I asked them one day before recess, "Why do you play Capture the Flag?"

"It's fun!" they chorused.

"What makes it fun?" I asked.

Their answers included that it was fun to run fast and catch people, it was fun to figure out ways to outsmart the other team, and it was fun when teammates helped each other escape.

Using the children's own words, I then asked, "So what can you do to figure out who will be flag guard in such a way that Capture the Flag can be fun for everybody and you can run fast, try to outsmart the other team, and help teammates?" Though I worded it as a question, I had in effect articulated a vision statement for the students. This vision reminded them—through their own words, no less—that their original reason for playing the game was to have fun. That larger vision allowed the children to put their individual squabbles in perspective and contribute constructive ideas for figuring out who would be flag guard.

FORMULATING EFFECTIVE VISION STATEMENTS

For most of us, vision statements don't roll spontaneously off the tongue. The most effective envisioning language, however simple and straightforward sounding, requires thought and planning. Remember, too, that as with all skillful teacher language, adopting effective envisioning language takes practice. If your vision statements don't come off sounding as polished as you'd like at first, be patient with yourself. In time your language will improve.

Generally, there are three steps in formulating an effective vision statement:

1. Think about your values or students' values as they relate to the situation at hand.

2. Articulate to yourself a specific and concrete goal that reflects this value.

3. Talk about these aspirations with ideas and words that engage children.

For example, Ms. Marks, the reading teacher above who hoped students would love reading so much that they'd rather read than watch

TV, began by identifying "becoming good readers" as a value. Then, she articulated to herself the specific goal of all the children "improving their reading ability by at least one grade level, and hopefully more." She realized, however, that those words would not mean much to the children and likely would not get them excited about working on their reading.

To shift to ideas and words that would be more meaningful to the children, Ms. Marks asked herself, "What would be happening from the students' point of view if they were to become better readers?" After consideration, she concluded that they would be able to decode a lot more words with a lot less effort. They would be able to read an entire story and really understand it. Not only that, if they were to develop their greatest potential as readers, they would be enjoying the story as they read it and looking forward to reading other books. They would see reading as something that's fun and useful to them and believe that the effort it takes to learn to read better is worthwhile. In fact, they would choose to read books in place of doing other things they loved to do. And what's something they love to do? Watch TV, of course!

This sequence of thought helped Ms. Marks develop her final statement for the children: "My hope is that by the end of this year you will all be book lovers! I hope each of you discovers at least one book that you love so much, sometimes you'd rather read it than watch TV!" Watching TV was something the children could grasp, and the idea of wanting to read rather than watch TV was surprising and compelling to them. These words, therefore, were successful in generating their commitment to becoming better readers.

IDEAS AND WORDS THAT ENGAGE CHILDREN

Clearly, the success of vision statements depends on expressing them through ideas and words that speak to the children. Here are some tips for achieving this critical step:

* Name positive identities for children.
* Use concrete images and words that children use.

* Try using metaphors.
* Let children fill in the details.

NAME POSITIVE IDENTITIES FOR CHILDREN

On the first day of school, a first grade teacher tells her eager but somewhat anxious group, "I see that our classroom is full of good thinkers who are ready to learn! This year, I expect that all of you will find some schoolwork that you'll be able to do easily and some that will require hard work. But we're all good thinkers, so we're all going to learn a lot!"

Naming the students as "good thinkers who are ready to learn" adds power to this vision because it gives the students an important, enticing identity. "Yes, we are good thinkers," they repeat in their heads. "We are ready to learn." Thus primed, the children now indeed are ready to learn.

But the strength behind this teacher's naming of the children as "good thinkers" is not just that it's a label the children like, but also that she speaks from deep conviction. She truly believes that all children are good thinkers in different ways and that all children begin school eager to succeed as learners. Yet she shares this belief not by talking in terms of differentiated instruction or multiple intelligences, but in simple terms that the children can understand and will find meaningful.

In another example, a third grade teacher, observing that the students were often distracted and inattentive during group discussions, decided to use envisioning language to inspire a change in the children's behavior. "We can do our best learning when we are careful listeners," he told the class. "What do careful listeners do?" Rather than explain the importance of listening or reprimand the children for not listening, this teacher sets a clear and positive goal by naming the children as potential "careful listeners." When children hear this identity named, they're likely to become intrigued and want to live up to this image of themselves.

There are a couple of things to watch out for when naming positive identities for children. One is inadvertently comparing the positive identity with a negative one. "I'm hoping for hard workers instead of lazy workers," I found myself telling children once. Without meaning to, I implied that perhaps I currently see the students as lazy. Once named, a negative label may carry more weight than a positive one, regardless of which one we intend to emphasize. Once they hear the negative label, students may have a hard time imagining themselves with the positive identity. Or they may become resentful and unwilling to work toward the positive vision.

Another caution is to avoid inadvertently naming stereotyped or divisive identities. A teacher once shared a vision of the class as "Boys and girls, skaters and jocks, all being friendly to each other." His intention was noble, but his words undermined the ideal of an inclusive community. By naming the students as separate groups, this teacher reinforced the very divisions he wanted to overcome. Far more effective would have been a simple sentence such as "In this classroom, everybody will feel welcomed and included by everybody else."

USE CONCRETE IMAGES AND WORDS THAT CHILDREN USE

When we teachers say that we want children to be respectful of each other, to be responsible learners, or to be motivated students, we may have a vivid mental picture of what such terms look like in action and a clear sense of why they're important. But children often don't. Abstract terms such as "respectful," "responsible," and "motivated" don't automatically paint clear pictures in students' minds. To be most effective, envisioning language needs to include concrete images and words that children themselves use daily. Ms. Marks talking about TV, the science teacher saying she hopes students will solve mysteries of "how things work," my asking students how they can choose a flag guard in a way that will "be fun for everybody" and allow them to "run fast, try to outsmart the other team, and help teammates"—these are all examples of using images and words that are meaningful to students.

One way to ensure that we're using language that works for students is to ask them why something is important and then draw on their words. An art teacher, bothered by the sixth graders' chronic put-downs of each other, told them, as she had many times before, that they should stop this behavior and be more respectful. The students responded cyn-ically, as they had many times before: "That's what all the adults in this school say. 'Be respectful, blah, blah, blah.' They're always saying that! We're tired of hearing about 'Be respectful.' The teachers, they just want you to be quiet and never have fun!"

Rather than ignoring the students' gripes or attempting to explain her point of view yet again, this teacher decided it was time for a differ-ent approach. She allowed the complaints to lead her to the students' genuine values and ideals. "You're tired of that word, 'respectful,'" she affirmed. "Seems like the teachers use it a lot just to make you listen to them." Then she asked for the students' thoughts and words. "What if 'respectful' really did mean something important to you? What would be happening for you at school if you genuinely felt respected by each other?"

"We'd just feel okay instead of mad at someone," one student explained. Another said, "We'd feel okay just being who we are and wearing the clothes we want to wear, and saying what we want to say." "And no one would be picking at us, trying to make us feel bad even if they think different," another student offered.

After reflecting on this information for a day, the teacher named a vision that used many of the students' words. "Everyone here has a right to feel okay about themselves," she said. "When you're in this class, each of you should be able to feel okay about what you wear, the work you do, and what you look like. What needs to happen so everyone can feel okay when they're here?"

Suddenly the students were alert. They sat up straighter, leaned for-ward, and began to raise hands to share their ideas. These were issues they cared deeply about and had thought about often. Together, the teacher and the class began the work of filling in the details of this exciting shared vision—the first step in bringing it to life.

TRY USING METAPHORS

Metaphors, such as the one with the spyglass that opened this chapter, can add clarity and power to envisioning language. "What do you see through the spyglass?" I have asked children after reading this story to them. "Let's pretend we're looking through magic spyglasses at our classroom. We're looking at our classroom when it's a safe and welcoming place for everybody and we're all doing our best learning. What kinds of things do you see? What are you doing?"

The spyglass metaphor excites the children's imaginations. They look through their imaginary spyglasses to see themselves as accomplished readers, friendly workers, or mathematicians. The playfulness of the metaphor encourages positive emotions about these self-images and makes our shared vision more real and compelling.

In my work with teachers, I have seen them use many different metaphors to make visions exciting for children. They include taking a journey, building a bridge, rowing a boat together, and weaving a colorful blanket. Effective metaphors may come from the literature we're reading with our class, the history topics we're studying, or other aspects of the curriculum and classroom life. For example, if we read the story of Miss Rumphius (Cooney 1982/1985), who planted lupine seeds to make the world more beautiful, we can use "planting our lupines" as a metaphor for interacting in ways that make the world a better place. A group of fifth graders studying early American explorers imagined themselves "seeking El Dorado" as they undertook challenges to reach their shared vision. Some great metaphors simply come from our own thoughts and experiences. Gardeners might use the metaphor of growing a garden. Football fans might use the metaphor of going for the Super Bowl.

My colleague Chip Wood used the metaphor of "climbing the mountain" when he wanted to share a vision of taking on a worthy challenge with his fourth and fifth graders. When they planned a field trip, he opened a discussion of ways to take care of themselves and each other in unfamiliar surroundings by saying, "You are ready to take another step up the mountain." When it was time to grapple with the issue of hurtful gossip, he told them again, "We are going to climb a little higher up the mountain." This metaphor made the children want that sense of accomplishment that comes from taking on and meeting a challenge. It also reminded the children that growing stronger and wiser is something that's accomplished in stages, step by step, not all at once. We climb a little higher, then we rest. Then we climb some more. We know that if we keep climbing, eventually we will reach the top.

LET CHILDREN FILL IN THE DETAILS

Visions become reality only when we engage in behaviors that bring them to life. The kingdom's fields become lush with crops only if the people till the soil, sow seeds, and irrigate. Children will become class experts on their research topics only if they spend the time reading about their topic, asking questions, writing draft reports, and listening to classmates' feedback. Before we arrive at these actions, we often need to imagine some details in our vision first: "What does being a class expert look and sound like? What would I be doing if I were an expert on my topic?" The answers to these questions would lead me to know what actions I'd need to take to become an "expert."

Teachers could simply name these details and dictate the actions, but children will be much more motivated if they're given the chance to come up with these specifics themselves. Not only does this help them clarify the vision, but it brings them in as co-creators of it. Allowing children to fill in the details also shows that their teacher has faith in their good ideas. Many teachers, therefore, follow with a question after articulating a vision statement.

For example, after Ms. Marks stated the vision that the first graders would love reading so much they'd sometimes rather read than watch TV, she asked them, "Imagine a book that you could love so much that you'd rather read it than watch TV. What might you find in such a book?" One child might imagine a book about race cars as one that she could love this much. Another might imagine a book with stories about animals or with puzzles to solve. The children can then actively look for books that fit their own mental picture and start reading.

After the third grade teacher told the class, "We can do our best learning when we are careful listeners," he asked, "What do careful listeners do?" As the children offer their ideas, they and the teacher together establish a vision for how they would behave to bring their identity of "careful listeners" to life.

Here are some other examples: "What would be happening on our field trip if everyone were having fun and learning?" "What would a math group that you'd enjoy be like? What would you see and hear? How would you feel?" "What would be happening for you at school if you genuinely felt respected by each other?"

Although the questions are often specific to the particular vision being shared, they fall into a few general patterns:

* What might you be doing if this were to come to pass?

* What kinds of things would be happening?

* How could you make this happen?

* What would you need for this to happen?

In addition to talking about these specifics, children can also draw or dramatize them. This allows children to think and express ideas in modalities besides those that rely strictly on verbal skills.

Whatever the method of expression, what's important is to let the children fill in the details of the vision, rather than explaining, illustrating, and describing them ourselves. The more we talk and explain, the less children are able to think. When we allow them the space to think, they come up with details and actions that inspire them—details and actions that can make their vision real.

SUMMARY

Like adults, children are more likely to meet hard challenges when they can see an exciting vision of themselves being successful. Using envisioning language, teachers can lift students out of their current reality to imagine themselves achieving in bigger, grander ways. Envisioning language can be used to motivate students as they start an endeavor—a new year, a unit of study, a project, or a reading period—or to help students solve day-to-day problems from disrespect during discussions to boredom with an assignment. Such language is most successful when it connects students' schoolwork with what they care most about in their larger lives. Once they have such a meaningful vision in their heads, children can begin to do the work of turning the vision into reality.

WORKS CITED

Adler, Alfred. 1958. *What Life Should Mean to You*. New York: G.P. Putnam's Sons.

Cooney, Barbara. 1982/1985. *Miss Rumphius*. New York: Penguin Puffin Books for Young Readers.

Deci, Edward L. and Richard Flaste. 1995. *Why We Do What We Do: Understanding Self-Motivation*. New York: Penguin Books.

Dreikurs, Rudolf, Bernice B. Grunwald, and Floy C. Pepper. 1998. *Maintaining Sanity in the Classroom: Classroom Management Techniques*. 2d ed. Philadelphia: Taylor and Francis.

Evans, Richard Paul. 2000. *The Spyglass: A Story of Faith*. New York: Simon & Schuster Books for Young Readers.

Kegan, Robert and Lisa Laskow Lahey. 2001. *How the Way We Talk Can Change the Way We Work*. San Francisco: Jossey-Bass.

CHAPTER THREE

Open-Ended Questions: Stretching Children's Academic and Social Learning

T he previous chapter talked about how teachers can use language to stretch children's visions of themselves, helping them see themselves achieving something grander than their current reality. Teachers can also use language to stretch children's curiosity, reasoning ability, creativity, and independence so that they learn more broadly and deeply. One of the most effective ways to do this is to ask children open-ended questions.

Open-ended questions are those for which there is no single right or wrong answer. Any reasoned and relevant response to an open-ended question is a good answer. Open-ended questions draw on students' own thoughts, knowledge, skills, experiences, and feelings. They encourage children to be inquisitive and to seek answers to satisfy their wonderings. The following classroom scene, in which the open-ended questions are set in italics, demonstrates an effective use of open-ended questioning:

A class is about to begin reading a new story, and the children have their books open to the first page. To generate interest in the story and gain some initial information about the children's knowledge of the vocabulary in it, the teacher, Ms. Nunn, asks a series of open-ended questions. She begins with, "Before we start reading, take a look at just this page. *What interesting words do you see?*" After a few quiet moments, hands go up.

"Castle!" shouts Raymond. "Castles are cool! I have a model castle."

"I can tell that's an important word for you, Raymond. *What clues does this word give you about what the story might be about?*"

"Knights? Usually castles have kings and knights."

"Maybe it's a fairy tale," Keira adds.

"Hmm. Interesting," Ms. Nunn muses. *"What makes you think it might be a fairy tale?"*

After the children have shared some thoughts on the nature of fairy tales, Ms. Nunn brings them back to the original question. *"What are some other interesting words on this page?"* she asks.

"A . . . sh . . . ashamed!" Myra decodes triumphantly. "I figured it out!"

"You certainly did!" Ms. Nunn agrees. *"How did you do that?"*

Myra explains how she recognized the "sh" blend. "Then I saw the 'a' and I thought 'asha,' and that made me think of 'ashamed.' Then I saw the letters matched the sounds for 'ashamed.'"

Ms. Nunn replies, "You used some good thinking there! *What's interesting to you about that word?"*

"Well, first I was interested just because I didn't know what it said," Myra replies.

"It's kind of like having a puzzle to solve," the teacher says, nodding.

"Yep. But now I think it's interesting that someone is going to be ashamed in this story."

"Someone might feel ashamed because they did something bad," Ethan asserts. "So someone is probably going to do something bad."

"You've thought of a good question for us to bring along with us as we read, Myra. Some kids are already getting some ideas about this. It'll be interesting to find out who is ashamed and why. *What other interesting words have folks found?"*

"Milkmaid," offers Arnie. "What's a milkmaid?"

"Hmm, what might a milkmaid be? Any guesses?"

"My grammy has a story about a milkmaid she tells me. It's a girl and she works hard and she's poor."

"Oh, those might be some clues," says the teacher. "The word itself may give you some more clues. Can you find the smaller words in the compound word?"

The conversation continues with the children deeply involved in sharing their ideas. By the time the discussion ends fifteen minutes later, the group has talked about context clues, compound words, historical jobs and roles, differences between fairy tales and historical fiction, gender roles, and more. The students have been prompted to think, share their knowledge, analyze information, and make connections among ideas. Their interest in the story grew. The teacher, meanwhile, learned a great deal about what her students knew. Much of this richness was due to the fact that Ms. Nunn used open-ended questions to move the discussion along.

WHAT MAKES OPEN-ENDED QUESTIONS SO POWERFUL?

Open-ended questions are powerful because they support the natural way children learn, they promote children's engagement, they encourage self-control, and they nurture a sense of community among classmates.

SUPPORTING THE NATURAL WAY CHILDREN LEARN

Educational theorists tell us that learning consists of a cycle. (Dewey 1938/1963; Piaget 1923/1959) The cycle begins with children initiating concrete activities based on ideas and goals they generate themselves. For example, after a child watches some older children playing soccer, he gets the idea that he'd like to learn to play soccer, too. This is a self-generated goal.

In the next step of the learning cycle, children actively explore, trying out materials and ideas and solving problems that come up. The child who wants to learn soccer, for example, finds some way to try it out, perhaps by kicking a soccer ball around the yard himself or by getting one of the older children to teach him.

In the final step of the learning cycle, children reflect back on their explorations and make sense of them. In the soccer example, this is when the child, after kicking the ball around for a while, stops to think, "Wow, I can kick that ball between those two trees from way back here! I couldn't do that before" or "The ball goes far, but my toe hurts from all that kicking."

When the children do this reflection, they incorporate their newly gained experiences into their understanding of how the world works. This new understanding generates more ideas and new goals, and the cycle starts again. For example, the child in the soccer example might decide to see if he can kick the ball between the two trees from an even farther distance, or if kicking the ball with a different part of his foot will solve the ouchy toe problem. As children go through this cycle again and again, their thinking and knowledge become more and more sophisticated.

Rich learning can result when children are allowed to experience this kind of natural learning cycle in the classroom, and open-ended questions vitally support this process at every stage, as the following graphic shows:

Open-Ended Questions and the Learning Cycle

Examples of open-ended questions that can prompt and encourage children at each stage of their natural learning cycle

Generating ideas and goals:

"What are some different ways you might test the strength of these materials?"

"What do you notice about this map? What kinds of things might you learn from it?"

"How could you figure out the answer to this problem?"

Reflecting upon their experiences:

"What did you like about your presentation?"

"What was hard about that? What made it hard?"

"What did you learn?"

"What would you do differently if you did this again?"

Actively exploring, experimenting, problem solving:

"How else could you sort those rocks?"

"What might help?"

"How does this compare with that?"

"What do you think will happen next?"

PROMOTING CHILDREN'S ENGAGEMENT

When we ask children "What do you want to try?" or "What might work?" or "What do you know about this?" we show trust in their ability to have good ideas, to think for themselves, and to contribute in valuable ways to the class. In other words, we help them feel a sense of autonomy, competence, and belonging—feelings that lead children to become engaged and to invest deeply in the activities of the class-room. (Deci and Flaste 1995)

In addition, children's responses to open-ended questions tell us what they know and understand so far about a topic or process. This tells us where to start with our instruction. When we start with what children know and are ready to learn next, and then build from there, children are more likely to be successful, to take risks to learn, and to support each other in taking risks—all of which make learning more fun and interesting.

In a classroom rich with open-ended questioning, children talk more than the teacher. That's a good thing, because when children talk in response to such questions, they're thinking. They're using analysis, syn-thesis, prediction, comparison, association, evaluation, and creativity. They make information meaningful to themselves. This is true active learning.

ENCOURAGING SELF-CONTROL

Open-ended questions help children gain confidence in themselves and become aware of how their choices affect themselves and others. For example, the question "What did you do that helped you learn these words?" prompts students to reflect on the fact that they learned the words as a result of something they did, and it pushes them to realize what it was they did that was effective. This self-confidence and self-awareness are essential to the development of true self-control, because exercising true self-control means choosing how we act based on a conscious awareness of the effects of our actions.

NURTURING A SENSE OF COMMUNITY

When we ask a child, "What made you decide to study this animal?" or "What's one interesting thing that you've learned about China?" the teacher and child are not the only ones who learn something about the child's interests and experiences. The other children in the room get a glimpse into the student's personality, too. This kind of learning happens with all kinds of open-ended questions: When children answer questions about their feelings and perceptions, the class is exposed to diverse points of view, which allows them to practice empathy. And when students hear classmates' responses to questions about their studies, they learn curriculum content from each other.

All this information allows students to make connections among themselves. The result is they're more likely to form genuine friendships, to appreciate one another's strengths, to value their differences, and to see themselves as a community.

WHEN TO USE OPEN-ENDED QUESTIONS

Open-ended questions can be used in many classroom situations, including when introducing a lesson or activity, during or at the close of a lesson or activity, and when solving a behavioral issue.

In each classroom situation, there can be a range of purposes for using open-ended questions:

* To increase students' awareness of what they know about a topic or process

* To generate interest in a topic or activity

* To encourage children to make personal connections to content they're learning

* To let children hear classmates' ideas and explore different perspectives

* To help identify any problems that may come up or clarify what the problem is when a child is struggling

* To generate possible solutions to a problem

* To plan the next steps in a project or process

* To help children evaluate their plan or process

The following table shows examples of open-ended questions for each of these purposes in various classroom situations. Note that many of the examples can also be used in situations other than the ones they're listed under. For example, it may be just as appropriate to ask "How did you figure that out?" during a lesson (on estimating in math, for instance) as it would be during problem solving around a behavioral issue (such as how to apologize for a hurtful comment).

SAMPLE QUESTIONS FOR DIFFERENT PURPOSES

	CLASSROOM SITUATION		
	Introducing a lesson or activity	**During and at the close of a lesson or activity**	**Solving behavioral problems**
Increasing awareness of knowledge	"What do you know about [birds, fairy tales, folk songs, basketball, rivers, etc.]?" "Where have you heard or read about this topic before?"	"What have you learned so far?" "How does this [map, letter, phrase, etc.] compare to that one?" "How could you put that into your own words?"	"What happened?" "What did you notice?" "How might an observer describe what happened?" "What would be an example?"
Generating interest	"What do you notice about [this poem, this ball, this book, etc.]?" "What do you wonder about when it comes to this topic?"	"What part of this do you find most interesting?" "What else might you want to try?" "What more would you like to know about this?"	"What questions do you have?" "What surprised you?" "What do you notice that's new to you?"

The leftmost vertical label reads: **PURPOSE**

	CLASSROOM SITUATION		
PURPOSE	**Introducing a lesson or activity**	**During and at the close of a lesson or activity**	**Solving behavioral problems**
Making personal connections	"How do you feel when you [hear a fairy tale, try a new sport, etc.]?" "When have you used [a microscope, rules, comparisons, etc.] before?" "When might you use [a song, this game, journal writing, etc.] to help you learn something?"	"What about this is especially interesting to you?" "How might this information help you [when you need to find a book, the next time you take the subway, when we visit the nature center]?" "What part would you especially want to remember?"	"What does this remind you of?" "How have you seen people use this skill?"
Hearing classmates' ideas	"How might we use [the computer, the microscope, etc.] to help us learn about [minerals, adjectives, great paintings, etc.]?" "What could you do if you forget the directions?"	"What are some ways you all figured that out?" "What are some questions you might ask when you do your interviews? Let's see how many ideas we can come up with as a class." "What are some possible ideas?"	"What are some possible reasons why people [call names, tease, don't finish work, etc.]?" "How does this compare to your experience? Let's hear from all of you."
Identifying or clarifying problems	"What problems could possibly come up when you do this?" "What might be hard for some people?"	"How's it going?" "Where are you stuck?" "How would you describe the problem?" "How could you possibly find out?"	"What's an example of this kind of problem?" "Where else do you see this problem happening?" "What might be going on in some kids' minds when they think about this?"

	CLASSROOM SITUATION		
PURPOSE	**Introducing a lesson or activity**	**During and at the close of a lesson or activity**	**Solving behavioral problems**
Generating possible solutions	"What could you do if [you think you're running out of time, you're stuck for ideas, etc.]?" "When would be good times to ask for help?"	"Which [book, color, eraser, block, etc.] do you think might work better for you?" "What might help?" "Where could you look for ideas?"	"How might someone solve that problem?" "Who could help?" "What else might work?"
Planning next steps	"How will you make sure to [finish on time, do every step, take care of each other, etc.]?" "What materials do you need to gather before you start?"	"What's your plan?" "What might someone's next move be?" "What's one thing you might do first?"	"What might a kid in that situation do differently next time?" "What might you do next?" "Which step feels like the right one to try first?"
Evaluating a plan or process	"How long do you think you will need?" "How will you decide whom to work with?"	"Why might some students choose this [strategy, object, tool, etc.] over the others?" "What's working for you?" "What's hard for you?"	"What might be a good way to know if your plan is working?" "How could someone know if this is their best work?" "What helped you concentrate well today?"

Should Teachers Stop Asking Closed-Ended Questions?

Absolutely not. Closed-ended questions, sometimes called "recitation questions," are questions for which there is a predetermined correct answer. These have a role in teaching. While teachers can enhance children's learning by asking open-ended questions in many classroom situations, there are also times when closed-ended questions are appropriate. Here are some examples:

* To discover students' knowledge and comprehension of facts
  "In what year was the Declaration of Independence signed?"
  "What are the stages in the water cycle?"

* To get specific needed information
  "Who brought the snack today?"
  "Which of you will do your presentation first?"

* To remind children of established procedures
  "What are you supposed to be doing right now?"
  "How do you score a point?"
  (See Chapter 6 for more about reminding language.)

* To confirm agreement
  "Are you ready to begin?"
  "Do you agree that the pattern here is they're all two-digit numbers?"

What's important is to distinguish between the purposes of closed-ended questions and those of open-ended questions, and then use the type most beneficial to the situation at hand. For example, if we want to generate students' interest in studying snakes, an open-ended question such as "What do you know so far about snakes?" is more likely to achieve our goal than a closed-ended question such as "What class of animal does the snake belong to?" On the other hand, if our goal is to see if students can apply their knowledge of snakes to what they learned about classifying animals, then the closed-ended "What class of animal does the snake belong to?" would be very appropriate.

ASKING EFFECTIVE OPEN-ENDED QUESTIONS

One wonderful thing about asking a truly open-ended question is that we never know what we'll hear in response. When I ask children open-ended questions, sometimes I get predictable answers. But often I get answers that I've never thought of before. It's always exciting for me to hear ideas that stretch not only the students', but my, thinking. How satisfying to be creating knowledge together!

Following are suggestions for making open-ended questions effective. First I give a few essentials that apply whenever we ask any open-ended question, and then some strategies to consider when asking open-ended questions in specific situations.

ESSENTIALS THAT APPLY TO ALL OPEN-ENDED QUESTIONS

* Genuinely open up your curiosity.

* Clarify exactly what you're asking for.

* Use words that encourage cooperation, not competition.

* Watch out for pseudo open-ended questions.

Genuinely open up your curiosity

For open-ended questions to be effective, it's critical that we ask them with genuine curiosity about students' thinking. Once I asked a group of fourth graders, "How might you use the colored pencils to show what you know about butterflies?"

"You could draw a butterfly and show the different parts," one child said. Others suggested, "You could make a map of Monarch butterflies' migration paths," "You could make a chart of the life cycle of a butter-fly," and, "You could draw and label different kinds of butterflies." Then, without missing a beat, a student offered, "You could write a story about the life of a butterfly and use different colors for different times in its life."

This last answer truly surprised me; it was something I never would have thought of. I don't know if the student—or any member of the class—realized that this answer was unusual or somewhat unlike the others. What I'm convinced of, though, is that if I had not felt and conveyed genuine curiosity in whatever reasoned and relevant ideas students had, that child probably would not have felt free to think creatively to come up with that idea. And it was a great idea. Sure, we could write the life cycle story of a butterfly in different colors! Why not? Our butterfly projects were richer and students' learning stretched because of the many ideas, including this one, that class members offered.

Being truly curious of children's responses also means valuing their thinking processes—focusing as much on how they arrived at their answers as on the answers themselves. If any reasoned and relevant response to an open-ended question is a correct one, then it follows that the reasoning children use matters.

For example, when the student suggested that we could write the life cycle of a butterfly using a different color for each stage, she demonstrated independent, logical, and creative thinking. It was this, not just the fact that the class now had an additional way of doing the assignment, that made her response valuable. As a teacher, when I ask children what they notice about something, I hope to promote careful observation and analysis. I therefore value any response that shows these kinds of thinking. When I ask students how people might feel or why they might behave in certain ways, I value any response that shows consideration of different points of view.

Children can tell when their teachers are genuinely interested in their ideas. If we're truly interested, over time children learn to trust that we really do want to know what and how they think. When they know this, they're more willing to reason and reflect, they gain more practice in thinking for themselves, and gradually they become more skillful, creative thinkers.

Clarify exactly what you're asking for

Suppose when I asked, "How might you use the colored pencils to show what you know about butterflies?" a child had answered, "You could pretend that the colored pencils are butterflies and make a play about them." Making such a play would have met the goals of this lesson, and in terms of the question I asked, this response is just as valid as the others. However, having students "fly" colored pencils around the room was, because of the potential chaos and safety issues, more than I wanted to deal with.

Fortunately, no student really gave such an answer. But the way to proactively prevent such a response would have been first to clarify to myself the boundaries of what the children are to think about, and then articulate these boundaries to the children. The resulting wording might have been "How could you use these colored pencils to *draw or write* something that shows what you know about butterflies?" This is still an open-ended question; it just has boundaries based on what I felt were appropriate options for student activities.

EXAMPLES OF ARTICULATING BOUNDARIES IN OPEN-ENDED QUESTIONS

Instead of:	Try:
"How could you use the globe?"	"How could you use the globe to discover facts about continents?"
"What kinds of things might you do on the field trip?"	"What kinds of things might you do on the field trip that will help you learn and keep you safe?"
"What are some ways you could solve that problem?"	"What are some ways you could solve that problem using the supplies in our classroom?"

Often we ask a question and then realize afterward that we haven't articulated the necessary boundaries. That's okay. We can always add the boundaries as a further clarification. Mr. Higa, a fifth grade teacher, heard himself asking the class, "What do you notice about this story?" then quickly realized that he didn't want to hear simply any observation the children had. He wanted them to notice the way the story resembled the last story they had read together. So he quickly added, "I'm looking for some ways this story is like the one we read last week. Let's hear some ideas."

There are times when teachers do want broad responses. In those cases, alerting students to that expectation can also be helpful. For example, if Mr. Higa had wanted any and all observations about the story, he could have clarified with a simple statement: "Let's see how many different things this group can notice about this story."

Use words that encourage cooperation, not competition

Sometimes an open-ended question leads to a competition among students to see who can give the best answer. While there is a place for competition in certain school arenas, usually when teachers use open-ended questions to facilitate discussions, the goal is for students to collaborate and learn from and with each other. A series of studies has demonstrated that competition among students decreases their intrinsic motivation to engage fully in activities. (Deci and Flaste 1995) Though some students—those who feel they have a chance to "win"— may be motivated by competition, many students will simply stop trying because it feels bad to lose. In the long run everybody loses, because everybody has lost the contributions of those who do not participate.

To keep a discussion from turning into a competition, one key step is to phrase the original question carefully. Questions that foster competition often, though not always, begin with "who" ("Who knows a good way to use clay?"); use words such as "better," "best," or "most" ("How can we make this graph the most beautiful?"); or somehow elevate some students above others ("Who has a better idea?"). While these may feel like very natural ways to talk, they assume that some answers will be better than others, and they encourage students to compete rather than collaborate. Here are some ways to rephrase questions to avoid creating an atmosphere of competition:

EXAMPLES OF DE-EMPHASIZING COMPETITION
WHEN ASKING QUESTIONS

Instead of:	Try:
"Who knows a good way to use the clay?"	"What are some different ways we might use the clay?"
"How can we make this graph the most beautiful?"	"What are some different ways to make this graph beautiful?"
"Whose drawing do you think is best? Why?"	"What good ideas do you see in the different ways people did their drawings?"
"Kerry, what strategies for writing neatly can you suggest to the others?"	"What strategies might help someone write more neatly?"
"Who has a better idea?"	"Who has a different idea?"

Watch out for pseudo open-ended questions

A pseudo open-ended question is one that sounds like an open-ended question but has behind it the teacher's desire to hear a certain answer. One year I had a student who loved magenta. Everything she colored, painted, or modeled in clay prominently featured magenta. Perhaps it was because I personally am not crazy about magenta, or perhaps it was because I wanted to buck—and get her to buck—the "girls are pink, boys are blue" stereotype, but one day, seeing another magenta-infused drawing, I asked her, "What do you think would happen if you used a different color?" It was only after the student replied, "I think I wouldn't like it as much," that I realized I had wanted her to say, "I think it would look better." It took me a moment to resist the urge to explain my thinking and to become genuinely curious about her thinking instead. "Oh? Why do you say that?" I gulped.

"This color stands out," she replied. "You can see it from far away, not like pink or yellow."

"*Not like pink,*" I repeated in my head. I had this student pegged all wrong, thinking she was going for pink (and its attendant "girly" stereotype) when she was going for standing out. Granted, she could have used other highly visible colors like royal blue or bright green; still, her explanation gave me insight into the thinking behind her work.

In this incident, it was fortunate that I caught myself after the student said "I think I wouldn't like it as much." I realized then that I was trying to give advice disguised as a question. But what if a teacher doesn't catch herself? An open-ended question will quickly shift to a closed-ended one, usually with poor results, if a teacher persists in fishing for the wished-for answer.

Take, for instance, the scene that opens this chapter. Suppose that when Ms. Nunn asked the children about interesting words on the page, she had wanted the children to discover two new vocabulary words: "magnificent" and "precious." When she asks, "What interesting words do you see?" many hands go up and Ms. Nunn calls on a happy-looking Raymond.

"Castle!" shouts Raymond. "Castles are cool! I have a model castle."

"Well, yes, but let's see what other interesting words you can find," Ms. Nunn responds with much less enthusiasm than Raymond. "There are some new words here that we're going to learn about. Do you see them?"

"A...sh...ashamed!" Myra decodes triumphantly. "I figured it out!"

"Oh, well, good for you, Myra," Ms. Nunn says flatly, and then, with pumped-up enthusiasm, "but there are some even bigger words. They will be our new vocabulary words. Who can see them?" Myra slumps in her seat.

By now the entire group is much less enthusiastic. Raised hands go down. The children have realized that Ms. Nunn is looking for a certain response, but they aren't sure what it is. Rather than risk joining the ranks of those who have gotten it wrong, they stop trying. Eyes wander and they begin to fidget. They don't know how to tell what their teacher is thinking.

When we ask pseudo open-ended questions, children soon realize that we are not really asking for their thoughts, knowledge, or perceptions, but ours. Many stop thinking at this point and become less engaged. Except for those children who are exceptionally self-confident,

Wait Time Adds to the Power of Open-Ended Questions

One way to make open-ended questions even more power-ful is to provide wait time—pausing a few seconds before taking students' responses. This pause gives all children a chance to think about the question before the discussion takes off. Students who tend to be slower to formulate answers will have a greater chance of being heard; those whose hands usually shoot up first will have the benefit of hearing some other perspectives before speaking. All stu-dents are likely to come up with more thoughtful responses. For more about wait time, see the sections "Know When to Be Silent" in Chapter 1 and "How to Listen: Two Technical Strategies" in Chapter 4.

students are likely to give up and simply wait for the teacher to give them the desired answer.

Another possible response from children is that they begin to guess at the "correct" answer. Many of us have experienced this scene, with students waving their hands wildly and almost desperately, and then giving answers that seem to have little thought behind them. If we're lucky—and it is a matter of luck—one student will finally hit upon the right answer, the one the teacher is looking for, and the lesson mer-cifully moves on. Or the teacher finally gives the children the right answer. Except for the one child who guessed the correct answer, the class is likely to feel uninspired or even dejected after such an interac-tion. Often the teacher is left discouraged as well. All would have turned out differently if the questioning had been truly open-ended and the teacher's intention truly to hear what was interesting to the students.

STRATEGIES FOR SPECIFIC SITUATIONS

In addition to these essentials, the following are some tips that could make the use of open-ended questions more effective in certain situations:

* Use words such as "might," "may," "could," or "possibly."

* Use words such as "some people" and "some kids."

* Specifically encourage multiple responses.

* Refer to concrete experiences.

* Choose words that cue thinking processes.

* Respond directly if students give jokey or edgy answers.

Use words such as "might," "may," "could," or "possibly"

Because closed-ended questions are the type most often heard in classrooms, many students have little experience answering truly open-ended questions. When we begin to ask such questions, children may not understand or trust that we really don't have a correct answer in mind. Still in the mode of "guess what's in the teacher's head," they may be afraid to voice their true ideas. In these cases, using words such as "might," "may," "could," or "possibly" can be helpful because we establish a greater sense of safety. "What might you do if you have a problem?" implies that the student is free to brainstorm, that we're just looking for possible ideas, and that the student will not be held to any answer he or she gives. "What will you do if you have a problem?" by comparison, either sounds like a test to see if the student knows the right answer (the one in the teacher's head), or implies that the teacher is asking the student for a decision or a commitment to a course of action. In either case it's more risky to answer a will question than a might question. In fact, some children won't know how to answer a will question before they've brainstormed and considered all the mights.

In the "Sample Questions for Different Purposes" table earlier in this chapter, notice how many of the questions contain the words "might," "may," "could," or "possibly." I've found that even students who are fairly experienced in answering open-ended questions often do more thinking and less self-censoring when I use this kind of tentative language. The result is that more ideas are generated.

Later, it may be appropriate for teachers to ask students to evaluate the various ideas and commit to one or a few of them. For example, a group of children are having difficulty completing homework. I begin by asking, "What might you do that could help you be sure to finish your homework?" After several different ideas are generated, I decide it's time for students to make a commitment. "Out of all these ideas, which ones do you think will work for you?" I ask. "Which will you do tonight?"

Use words such as "some people" and "some kids"

Related to using "might" and "may" is using impersonal nouns such as "some people" and "some kids"—for example, "What might some people find hard about doing homework?" rather than "What's hard for you about doing homework?" If children feel that their answers are seen as hypothetical—not necessarily reflecting their own views or experiences—they may feel safer sharing their ideas. This can be especially helpful with students new to answering open-ended questions, or when the conversation is about a sensitive topic such as a behavior issue or an academic area that the student is struggling with. Again, notice that many questions in the "Sample Questions for Different Purposes" table in this chapter use impersonal nouns.

Specifically encourage multiple responses

Another way to make sure children understand that we are not looking only for a few pre-determined responses is to specifically invite many responses. There are several ways to do this:

* Embed words such as "how many," "different," and "other" in the question.

    "How many different ways can you think of to . . . ?"
    "What are other possible reasons?"

* Follow the question with a challenge to name as many ideas as possible.

   "What do you think is going to happen to this character later in the story? Let's see how many different ideas we can come up with."

* Ask children each to think of a response.

   "What are some rules that will help us all do our best learning this year? I'd like each of you to think of a rule that you feel is important."

Here are some more examples of questions that specifically invite multiple responses:

* "We've got five good ideas here. Let's see if we can come up with three more."

* "What are some different ways animals might take care of themselves in the winter?"

* "Let's see if we can think of ten different adjectives that could describe the early settlers."

* "How many different ideas for a story topic can you think of?"

* "What's one way you might use these watercolors to paint a picture? What's another way?"

Refer to concrete experiences

Because children tend to be concrete thinkers, it can be helpful to ask them to think about something specific—a particular assignment, activity, or event rather than a general issue or idea, especially when opening a conversation. For example, asking Louise about the beaver dam model she just made ("What are some things you like about this dam?") is likely to be a more effective place to start than asking about a general category such as "your schoolwork." Louise probably will have an easier time thinking about how she learned about beaver dams and retrieving the details of creating the model now sitting in front of her than coming up with generalizations about her schoolwork.

If our goal is to have Louise reflect about schoolwork in general, we can guide her toward that once she has named some specifics—about the beaver dam, the explorer report, the weather chart, and other assignments. With the specifics named (and perhaps charted on paper), we might then ask, "What are some ways we can summarize these specifics?" to help guide Louise in drawing conclusions about her schoolwork in general.

EXAMPLES OF REFERRING TO CONCRETE EXPERIENCES

Instead of:	Try:
"How would you describe your writing?"	"What are some things you like about the character sketch you did of your sister?"
"What are some ways you could be a better student?"	"What did you do during today's partner share that helped you learn?"
"How do you feel about your math work?"	"What about this morning's math assignment makes you proud?"
"What do good scientists do?"	"What are some ways to be good scientists when we observe our worm farm today?"
"How do responsible people act?"	"What does it look like when people are responsible in the cafeteria?"

Choose words that cue thinking processes

Often children have an easier time responding to open-ended questions when we name the thinking process they'll need to use to answer the questions. Not only can this get their wheels turning, but it helps clarify our expectations. We can embed the cues in the question itself (for example, "What do you *predict* might happen next?") or add it as a direction after the question (for example, "What do you think might happen next? Make a *prediction*.") This strategy can be very effective as long as we've already taught the students what the named thinking process means and given them a chance to practice it.

Here are some examples of cuing students on thinking processes:

   * "Let's brainstorm for ideas about how to solve this problem."

* "What do you predict might happen to these plants?"

* "How might you compare the qualities of slate and marble?"

* "How could you evaluate which drawing is better?"

* "Why did the character make those choices? Make some educated guesses."

* "How might you get others to agree with you? Suggest a persuasive argument."

* "How did you help a classmate today? Describe one way."

Respond directly if students give jokey or edgy answers

Sometimes students respond to an open-ended question by saying something jokey or edgy, or perhaps sarcastic. Rather than getting pulled in, we can respond directly to their words and then quickly and firmly pull their attention back to the question we asked. By doing so, we maintain the focus and importance of the discussion.

For example, for a few days now, many students in the class have been struggling to get their work done. To help students figure out what might be causing the problem and what to do about it, I pull together a meeting and ask the class, "Why might someone have a hard time getting work done?"

"Because they're dumb?" Alicia replies with a smirk.

Taking her remark seriously, I say, "Sometimes when we find it hard to finish work, we can *feel* like we're dumb. But there's no one in this class who is truly unable to learn. So let's think of why it might be hard even though someone is not dumb, but rather perfectly able to learn."

Rather than respond to her "joke" as a challenge, I responded simply, directly, and empathetically, then quickly redirected her and the rest of the class to the original question at hand.

Here's another example: "What patterns do you see in this number grid?" Ms. Avon asks her third graders.

"I see a pattern of NUMBERS! Ha, ha!" Mike jokes.

"Mike, you've identified a very basic pattern. These are all numbers. What other patterns do people see here?" Ms. Avon says sincerely.

Ms. Avon did not laugh along with Mike, scold him for clowning around, or get pulled in to Mike's joking in any way. Instead, she responded simply and directly on face value and redirected everyone to the original question, thereby maintaining the focus of the discussion.

SUMMARY

Open-ended questions powerfully support children's academic and social learning by encouraging their curiosity and challenging them to think things through for themselves. Useful in a variety of classroom situations, open-ended questions can have a range of purposes, from helping students become aware of their knowledge to helping them generate solutions to problems. By keeping a true open mind and using careful phrasing, teachers can use open-ended questions to their full effect, bringing forth student responses that enlighten the student, classmates, and teacher.

WORKS CITED

Deci, Edward L. and Richard Flaste. 1995. *Why We Do What We Do: Understanding Self-Motivation*. New York: Penguin Books.

Dewey, John. 1938/1963. *Experience and Education*. New York: Collier MacMillan Publishing.

Piaget, Jean. 1923/1959. *The Language and Thought of the Child*. New York: The Humanities Press, Inc.

CHAPTER FOUR

Listening: Understanding the Message in the Words

R ecently a friend of mine told a story about a married couple who
lived in her neighborhood when she was a kid. The man was
Chinese and the woman Korean. The man, a gregarious sort, liked to
tell and retell stories to the neighbors about how he knew little Korean
and his wife knew little Chinese when they first got married, and the
humorous communication blunders that resulted. My friend would
laugh along with the adults and never gave much further thought to
these stories. The years passed, during which she went to school and
played with the couple's three children and the man's oft-repeated
tales became part of the comfortable background noise of that com-

munity. Then, as she reached her teenage years, slowly she began to think more deeply about the stories and to be amazed at how the couple—at how any two people—could share a life together when they didn't comfortably speak a common language. One day, when the man was again telling one of his anecdotes while the wife listened amusedly, my friend spoke up to ask seriously how they did manage to understand each other in those early years. She expected the couple to say they used sign language, they drew pictures, they consulted dictionaries a lot. Instead, they paused, looked at each other for a moment, and said, "We listened."

"Listened?" The answer puzzled my friend. It was decades later before she finally began to grasp the wisdom in that answer. So powerful is good listening that it can allow us to hear through considerable language barriers and understand the intended meanings behind each other's words. Granted, the couple grew more fluent in speaking each other's native language as the years passed, but it was listening that carried them through the earlier years and gave them enough understanding to set up a household, parent three young children, and tend to the myriad details of a shared life.

Fortunately, most U.S. teachers speak the same language as most of their students, and when there are non-English speaking children in the class, there may be adults or students who can help translate. And teaching a class is not the same as maintaining a marriage, to be sure. Even so, active, deep listening is as important in our classrooms as it is in the relationship in the story above. We have to listen to students in order to teach them well. If true listening can lead to the kind of understanding that allows a cross-language marriage to thrive, think what it can do for our understanding of students. Effective listening is an essential teaching tool—as important as other fundamentals such as careful observing, speaking, and modeling.

WHAT EXACTLY IS LISTENING?

Listening is more than passively receiving someone's words. It's searching for the speaker's intended meaning, which often requires paying attention to what's being said beneath the words. Listening therefore is a highly active undertaking. As poet Alice Duer Miller put it, "Listening is not merely not talking, though even that is beyond most of our powers; it means taking a vigorous, human interest in what is being told us." (Fitzhenry 1987)

How often, for example, do teachers hear students say "I don't care!"? If we listen well, we may pick up on the fact that they don't really mean they don't care. Depending on the tone of voice, the inflection, the context of the remark, and other signals, "I don't care!" may mean "I'm angry," "I'm afraid," "I'm confused," "I don't know," "This is too hard," or "I care but I'm saying I don't care because I want to appear cool."

To take a "vigorous, human interest" in understanding which meaning is behind "I don't care" and all the things our students say, we have to devote our full attention to the students while they're speaking, suspending for the moment our own agenda and point of view. This is hard, because most of us are in the habit of planning what we'll say next when someone's speaking. Perhaps we're afraid there will be an awkward silence after the person's words if we haven't planned what to say. Perhaps we're just used to hurrying. Or maybe we're afraid we'll forget our own point if we set it aside even momentarily. It helps to remind ourselves that silences are okay and even necessary, especially when talking with children, because children need that time to process all the verbal information that's being put forth. (See the section "Know When to Be Silent" in Chapter 1 for more details.) And we can reassure ourselves that if our point is important and still relevant after hearing what the student has to say, we will remember it.

Another possible reason it's so hard for us to suspend our own point of view is that doing so can feel like we're implying agreement with the speaker. But suspending is not the same as giving up forever. To listen to a student express his opinion on how a rule isn't fair or how a procedure should be changed does not mean agreeing with that opinion. It does mean fully understanding that opinion. After understanding, we can agree, disagree, open up the issue for a group discussion, or explain our reasoning for our position and hold firm to it.

Make no mistake, to communicate effectively we should actively consider how to respond to the speaker's words—but only after fully understanding them. Listening and responding to students is therefore a three-step process: First, we really take in their words. Second, we figure out the true intention of their words, looking at tone, context, and other signals for clues. And third, we think about how to respond.

This chapter will offer two strategies—pausing and paraphrasing—that can help teachers ensure that all three steps happen when communicating with students. But first, here's more on why, specifically, listening is so important to teaching.

WHY LISTEN?

What are the benefits of listening in teaching? The short answer is that listening tells us how to communicate most effectively with students, and it gains us entry into the students' world so we can influence their learning. The longer answer is that it does this through the following ways:

LISTENING LETS US KNOW THE CHILD

I firmly believe that knowing the children we teach—individually, culturally, and developmentally—is as important as knowing the content we teach. When we know students fully, we can make better decisions about curriculum, classroom management, and discipline that will fit their needs. Through careful listening, I learn that Trisha cares perhaps more than most children her age about appearing capable. This tells me that it might be best to give her any needed redirections in private. Listening to Ben's sharing about his weekend, I gather that he likes having choices of activities to do. I make a mental note that the classroom strategy of giving students some choices in their learning might be especially effective with him.

To be understood is also simply one of the most basic of human needs. We all need to feel understood to have a sense of belonging and significance. To be motivated to learn, children need to feel like they belong and are important in the classroom community. Listening is crucial in this equation because the best way to understand people is to listen to them.

WHEN WE LISTEN, CHILDREN LEARN ABOUT THEMSELVES

By listening to students and then reflecting back to them what we heard, we can help them become more conscious of their own interests, talents, worries, and questions. This self-awareness is essential if students are to learn at their best.

For example, Mr. Whitt listens as Brian, a highly social child, explains how he thought of his writing topic. "At first I was just gonna write about space invaders again so I could trade ideas with Mike and Taiki. But I'm getting kind of tired of that. Then I thought about how I really like my new dog and I thought it would be different and fun to write about that 'cause it's something real."

After pausing a moment to digest Brian's explanation, Mr. Whitt responds. "Ah, so you're changing how you choose topics? You're going from science fiction to nonfiction. And you also seem to be starting to look inside your own mind for topics that you really care about even if your friends are writing about something else."

Mr. Whitt's thoughtful paraphrase, possible only because of his careful listening, helps Brian become more aware of how he's changing the way he chooses a topic. Brian learns that he's expanding his writing interests and repertoire by trying a different genre. He becomes more conscious of the fact that he's thinking more independently and developing his own voice as a writer. This awareness of how he's growing as a writer will help Brian practice, reflect on, and build on his new-found skills.

LISTENING BUILDS A SENSE OF COMMUNITY

When we listen and reflect back to students what we understood, we also help the whole group of students get to know each other. When the class hears me say, "So, Jerome, it sounds like you're concerned about how the older students might act if you say that to them on the bus," and Jerome nods solemnly, they're gaining empathy for how Jerome feels. When they hear me say to Lily, "Your point, then, is that there are two ways to change the story's ending, and both would be fair to this character," they get a little insight into how Lily thinks. As students learn more about each other, they care more about each other and come to see themselves more as a community.

Just as powerfully, when I, as the teacher, listen to all students, I'm setting a standard and a tone of respect and empathy that are fundamental to a strong community. I'm showing that all students are worth listening to. Regardless of whether I agree with a child's remark, the remark is listened to and therefore respected. My careful listening also teaches students by example how to listen to each other, and when they do this, their community is strengthened.

LISTENING MAKES OUR QUESTIONING MORE EFFECTIVE

If we're going to ask children open-ended questions as discussed in the last chapter—or any questions, for that matter—it's important that we listen to their answers. Children can tell when we're not taking a deep interest in their answers, and they'll stop responding.

Suppose I say to Kyle, "You've shared three interesting facts about Cesar Chavez to the class. What else would you like to know about his life and work?" Kyle says something about Chavez and strikes. But I'm not sure what he said exactly because as he was talking, I was thinking about his mannerism in sharing and making a mental note about improvements he could make. I respond vaguely with, "Hmm, interesting," and Kyle wanders off with a somewhat dissatisfied look on his face. It's obvious to him that I hadn't fully engaged with his answer. One or two more times of this kind of response from me, and Kyle will stop engaging with my questions.

By contrast, if I'd listened attentively to Kyle, I would have understood that what he wanted to learn about was hunger strikes because he'd read on a website that Chavez did them and they weren't really like a "strike." I then might've said, "Sounds like you're interested in hunger strikes because they seem to be different from strikes where you make a point by refusing to work." I then could've helped guide Kyle in finding an explanation of what hunger strikes are all about. Feeling my engagement, Kyle would likely take my question seriously again the next time, and over time, develop trust in my genuine interest in his learning and consistently respond in earnest to my questions.

WHEN WE LISTEN, STUDENTS TAKE THEIR
LEARNING MORE SERIOUSLY

But what about the child who responds to our questions with jokes or sarcastic comments? If we listen carefully, we can usually hear a more serious message within most jokes and jabs. By responding directly to those, we elevate the conversation, inviting the student to engage in a more meaningful way. For example, asked to name some personal goals for the school year, Connor says, "Play computer games all day? HA HA!" Sensing a possible honest interest in computer games, the teacher says, "Oh, so you like computers? What do you like about them?" Connor's big grin shifts into a smaller smile as he detects the teacher's genuine tone. "They're fun. You can do things fast," he replies. "That's true," the teacher says. "Do you think you'd like to see what other fast things you can do on computers besides games?" "I guess," Connor replies after a moment. Eventually he arrives at "Learn more about computers" as a serious goal for the year.

In another example, Mr. Leon asks Alyce, "What will you write about today?" "I'm gonna write about … nothing!" Alyce grins. At this point, Mr. Leon is sorely tempted to tell Alyce, "Well, that's not a choice! You'd better get going on this assignment!" Instead, he pauses and takes a moment to consider his student's words as a genuine attempt to communicate rather than as a challenge to his authority. "Hmmm. Nothing … How would you write about nothing, Alyce?" Mr. Leon asks thoughtfully.

"Can't!" Alyce chirps.

"Oh! So you'd really rather not write at all right now!"

"Yep, that's right!"

"Well, did you know that even professional writers sometimes don't want to write or find it really hard to write? Would you like to hear some things that they say help them?"

Alyce looks surprised. "Yeah, I guess so," she says cautiously.

The same principle applies to all children's talk, not just their sarcasm or wisecracks. If we stop and really listen to what students are saying, even their casual chatter, they'll begin to take their own words more seriously. "My teacher cares what I think. Hmm. What *do* I think?" the self-talk might go. And when they question themselves like this, students are on their way to stretching their potential.

OUR LISTENING HELPS STUDENTS BECOME BETTER COMMUNICATORS

By listening and reflecting what we understood back to students, we can help them improve their communication skills. For example, during a discussion about the Revolutionary War, the conversation turns to how the colonists might have decided whether to side with the British government or with the American revolutionaries. Asha raises her hand to comment, somewhat inarticulately, "Some people don't like either way, like, they agree and don't agree." The teacher paraphrases, saying, "You seem to be making the point that people don't have to be on one side or the other, but can take a neutral stance."

Asha had an interesting idea, but it wasn't quite gelled, and she lacked the words to express it clearly. By paraphrasing her words as "don't have to be on one side or the other" and using the term "neutral stance," the teacher helped Asha clarify her idea and supplied some vocabulary that she can use to express it. "Yeah, neutral stance," Asha affirms. Later, in a small group discussion and in writing about the topic, Asha uses the term to good effect.

Note that reflecting what students said back to them in this way is not the same as voice-overs, something this book advises against in Chapter 1. In a voice-over, the teacher simply repeats, mechanically, something a student said and moves on. For example, suppose a teacher asks students for ways they could make a pattern with some art materials. "Red and blue," a student says, and the teacher says, "Red and blue. What else?" This is a voice-over. By contrast, when teachers reflect back through paraphrasing, they use words that are different from what the student said but that capture the student's intent, and they pause to check whether they've understood that intent correctly. Or they may wait until several children have offered ideas, then summarize—for example, "You're thinking about using different combinations of colors and objects to make patterns. Are there other ways you could create pat-terns?" This helps students crystallize and stretch their thinking. (For more, see the "Paraphrasing" section later in this chapter.)

Our listening also simply models for students how to be good lis-teners themselves—how to take in a speaker's words, how to search for the intended meanings in the words, and how to respond. These are key skills that make them more effective communicators.

How to Listen: Two Technical Strategies

Two concrete strategies that can help us listen more carefully are pausing and paraphrasing.

PAUSING

One of the best ways to become a better listener is to get in the habit of pausing—allowing some wait time—before responding to others' words. Knowing that there will be a pause to give us time to formulate a response frees us to attend fully to a student's comment. As stated in Chapter 1, researchers have found that pausing three to five seconds usually ensures better listening and more thoughtful responses. The pause allows us to think, "What am I hearing and seeing here? What's this child really trying to communicate? How can I best respond?"

For those not used to pausing, three to five seconds can feel quite long and awkward. It's no wonder, because in modern western culture, silence tends to be regarded as a problem, an embarrassing emptiness that needs to be filled. In actuality a pause, when used as intended, is already filled—with active thinking. Many of us also feel that our school days are so busy that we don't have time for pauses. This is an under-standable belief, but the truth is we don't have time not to pause. We can teach more and students can learn more if we pause.

So how do we get past the initial awkwardness? One way is to count. No need to try too hard at first to think all the right thoughts or ask ourselves any questions during the pause. We can simply count silently to five. If this feels strange, just remember that it's better to be count-ing than to be thinking about our own point of view. As pausing becomes more second nature, the counting will fade and we'll naturally begin to use the time to consider what the student said, what he or she intended, and only then, how we might respond.

After pausing, in many cases it may be enough to give a simple acknowledgement, such as eye contact, a nod, a thoughtful "Hmm …" or "Uh huh," a smile, or a "Yes." In this way we establish that the words are heard and stand on their own without a need for endorsement or clarification. They are valuable in and of themselves.

Sometimes these simple gestures or utterances aren't enough of a response. For example, if a student makes a suggestion and wants to know what we think of it, it wouldn't do to supply only a smile and a "Hmm …" What if, after pausing to think, we still aren't sure how to respond? It can help to have a set phrase to use in these situations. It can be as direct as "I want to think more about that." Later, when we've come up with something to say, we can get back to the student: "Shana, about your idea for our open house, …" Except for the minority of classroom situations that absolutely require an immediate response, this is a perfectly fine way to handle conversations with students.

It's important to remember to use these various kinds of acknowledgments consistently from student to student. If we respond effusively to some students and simply or not at all to others, we may appear to endorse or value students' comments unequally. Those students who think that their thoughts and words are less valued are then less likely to engage in discussions.

PARAPHRASING

Paraphrasing is restating the essence of a speaker's message in one's own words. While in many cases, simply acknowledging a student's words with a nod or short utterance such as "Uh huh" is most effective, paraphrasing is powerful when we're holding problem solving discussions, coming to agreements, making plans, or trying specifically to deepen mutual understanding of an issue.

Paraphrasing has three purposes:

* It encourages students to make sure what they said was what they really meant. As they do this, they often refine their ideas

and become more aware of their true thoughts and feelings. This can lead to greater self-control because children who know what they think and feel, and how to articulate it, are more able to make conscious decisions, evaluate those decisions, and learn from them.

* It allows teachers to make sure we've understood students correctly. Once students confirm that our understanding is accurate, we can go on to the next step, whether that's guiding them in developing their ideas further, sharing our own point of view, or doing nothing further for the moment. Besides preventing miscommunication, checking to make sure we've understood students correctly shows that we respect and value their thinking.

* It leads both the students and teachers to think more deeply and in more sophisticated ways about a topic. For students, this effect is especially pronounced when teachers follow paraphrasing with an open-ended question that prompts them to look at their idea in a new context or from another perspective.

Here are some ways to paraphrase effectively:

Use your own words

For teachers, paraphrasing shouldn't be a simple parroting of a few key phrases back to students, though this may be a place to begin when we're just learning this strategy. With practice, we can learn to restate the heart of students' messages in our own words. Depending on the situation, we can choose different ways to do this:

* Restate the main idea. "Matt, tell me about your writing," a teacher says. Matt replies, "I've got these robots and they can drive cars and fly planes and stuff. And everyone thought they were cool. But now they're taking over and there's this guy, Marcus. He's gotta stop 'em." After pausing, the teacher says, "So the people who made the robots gave them lots of skills, but now it's backfiring. Now you need a human hero." "Yeah!" Matt says.

We Can Teach Students to Pause, Too

In addition to developing a habit of pausing ourselves, we can teach our students this strategy as well. Early in my career I observed a mentor, Chip Wood, teaching children to listen to each other and then pause during class discussions. He taught them not to raise their hands during or immediately after someone spoke. It was only after the speaker was done and all had stayed quiet for a few seconds that those who wanted to could raise their hands for permission to speak. Once someone began speaking, all other hands went down and the focus was, once again, entirely on the speaker.

The effect of this simple strategy on class discussions was powerful. I could see that it helped everyone relax and listen to each other without fear that their own ideas would be cut off by the more aggressive speakers in the class. Quieter, less assertive children were more likely to be heard because they had time to think and formulate responses. The children became increasingly perceptive over the course of a discussion, their ideas building upon previously shared thoughts. Though the pace was slowed, the children shared more, and the variety and quality of their ideas were higher than in other groups I'd observed where pausing was not a standard practice.

* Name indirectly expressed feelings. Sometimes the feelings conveyed through body language and tone are the most important part of a message. Naming these feelings lets the student feel known and lets us check our understanding. "Tell me about your writing, Sandi," a teacher says. "I'm writing about my cousin. Her name is Amy and she's moving … " Sandi's voice trails off and she

looks down to hide her trembling lips and sad eyes. After a pause the teacher says, "Your cousin seems special to you. She's moving away and you're sad about that." "Mm hmm," Sandi murmurs.

* Organize thoughts into categories. This often gives children new insights, leading to a fresh round of ideas. "What are some things people in our class can do to make recess more fun for everybody?" a teacher asks. Students' suggestions include "If someone wants to be on a team, just let them," "Don't have secret clubs that leave people out," "If people want to be on teams they have to follow the rules," and "No cheating!" After pausing to consider these, the teacher says, "It sounds like there are two categories to think about: what people who are included in games can do to make recess better for others, and what people who aren't being included can do so that others want to include them. What else?"

* Name principles that tie ideas together. "What do you think will happen to the seed we put in the dirt and the seed we put in the wet towel?" a teacher asks. Students offer various ideas: "I think they'll both grow." "The seed in the dirt won't grow. It's too cold over there." "The seed in the wet towel will grow. The dirt is too dry." "They're both in the dark and I think seeds like to grow in the dark." The teacher pauses to take these in, then says, "Many of you are thinking about the conditions that help seeds grow, such as the temperature, the amount of light or darkness, and the amount of moisture. Let's keep thinking."

Avoid using "I"

Many of us have learned to begin paraphrases with "What I'm hearing you say is … " or "I'm understanding that … " This can inadvertently take the focus away from the student. Educators and consultants Robert Garmston and Bruce Wellman point out that referring to ourselves this way "signals to many speakers that their thoughts no longer matter and that the paraphraser is now going to insert his or her own ideas into the conversation." (Garmston and Wellman 1999, 40)

For example, if the teacher leading the discussion about what would happen to the seeds says, "So, what I'm hearing are considerations of the conditions that make seeds grow," the message changes subtly. The focus shifts to the teacher's perceptions and understandings rather than the children's. Some children might even wonder, "Is that what the teacher wants to hear? Did we do something wrong?"

Some alternatives to using "I" include "So you're saying … ," "You seem to be feeling [wondering, thinking, doing] … ," "Hmm. You're thinking about … ," and "You want us to know … "

Keep it brief

Brevity in paraphrasing helps keep the focus on the student rather than shifting it to our own thoughts and feelings. In the above examples, the paraphrases consist of one or two sentences. The fewer words we can use to convey our sense of students' messages, the better.

Use an approachable voice

This is important in all paraphrasing because the purpose of paraphrasing is to show that we have truly heard the speaker and want to make sure we understand the communication. But it's especially important for teachers to do this because we are in a position of power in relation to students. Our voice, combined with carefully chosen words, is key to helping students feel safe in communicating their true thoughts and feelings.

There are various ways to make our voice approachable; each teacher will find her or his own style. One common way is to inflect our tone as if asking a question. For example, "So you're saying that we need more details on what kind of food worms eat?" a teacher paraphrases, showing that the student is welcome to correct her restatement. Another way is to choose tentative words such as "seem" ("You seem to want your poem to express how you don't love snow") or "it sounds like" ("It sounds like this class has three different ideas"), and to use a gentle voice along with an open facial expression.

Follow paraphrasing with an open-ended question

Sometimes a pause and a paraphrase are all that's needed to help children continue to develop their ideas. Other times, once children confirm that we have truly heard and understood them, they may need an open-ended question to prompt them to think further.

For example, a teacher says, "Berry, tell me about your writing."

"I'm making a book about snakes," Berry says. "See, I drew a rattle-snake! I know they have diamond shapes on them. And I know about cobras and black snakes. A black snake bit me once! But it isn't poisonous. And there's garter snakes, water moccasins … There's lots of cobras in Florida."

The teacher pauses, then paraphrases: "You know about lots of different kinds of snakes. You also know some things about what different snakes do and where they live."

"Yeah. I really like snakes!"

Another brief pause, and the teacher says, "Yes, I can tell! What's most interesting to you about snakes?"

Without the teacher's open-ended question, Berry might have stayed in her mode of listing what she knows about snakes, without taking the more analytical step of identifying one aspect of snakes to focus on in her writing.

TEACHER INTENTION MAKES PAUSING AND PARAPHRASING WORK

Pausing and paraphrasing are useful techniques. But remember that it's the teacher's true intention to understand students that makes these technical strategies work. If we pause and paraphrase only for their own sake or use pauses and paraphrases as opportunities to think and talk about our own ideas, the techniques will lose their power. The pauses and paraphrases are then likely to feel and sound robotic, students will probably feel disrespected and not understood, and their learning is likely to stay flat. But if we pause and paraphrase in order to truly understand how students think and feel and what they're trying to communicate, these techniques will help elevate our teaching and enhance students' learning.

Pausing and Paraphrasing in Action

Below are examples of pausing and paraphrasing being used in various classroom situations. The examples show teachers using the techniques effectively. They also show students using pauses here and there. (While ideally students would pause after all comments from teachers and classmates, in reality their pauses are seldom so consistent. These examples show what's typical in students who are still learning to pause.)

During independent work time

Teacher: Danae, you've been really focused on your book. What's so interesting?

Danae (grinning): I just think it's really funny and interesting that a mouse can ride around on a motorcycle.

Pause

Teacher: So, you're intrigued with the fantasy part of it?

Danae: Yeah, I guess so. And also it's interesting to think about how a mouse would see the things that people think are just normal.

Pause

Teacher: Kind of gives you a different perspective, huh?

Danae: Yeah.

During individual problem solving

Teacher: Robert, I've noticed that you've been arguing a lot with some of the kids. What have you noticed?

Pause

Robert: Well, a little bit with Rudy and Maurice, I guess.

Pause

Teacher: Tell me more about that.

Robert: Rudy and Maurice are just always picking on me. They don't like me, so I don't like them.

Pause

Teacher: So it seems like Rudy and Maurice are being mean for no reason.

Robert: Yeah.

Pause

Robert: And sometimes I'm mean to them, too.

Pause

Teacher: Oh. So, you think sometimes they might have a reason?

Robert: Well, sometimes.

Pause

Teacher: Tell me more about when you are mean to them. What do you do?

DURING A GROUP DISCUSSION

Teacher: What are some things you know about deserts?

Pause

Manny: They're very dry and brown.

Pause

Samika: Lots of sand, I think.

Brianna: Some deserts have cactuses and they are green. Sometimes they have flowers.

Pause

Jerry: Deserts are deserts because they get hardly any rain. And they're hot.

Manny: Deserts can be cold at night. I was in a desert when it was cold.

Surea: Deserts can have flowers in them.

Pause

Leah: Deserts can have camels. And people who live in tents.

Pause

Teacher: So deserts are dry and sandy, but they also have plants and animals and even people in them. What else do you know or think you might know about deserts?

DURING GROUP PROBLEM SOLVING

Teacher: I've been noticing that lots of you are having difficulty getting your homework done on time. What might be some reasons that people have a hard time getting their homework done?

Pause

Alejandra: Sometimes the homework is too hard and they don't know how to do it.

Pause

David: If you can't do it and you don't have anyone to help you, it's hard.

Rickie: I have to go to my Grandma's after school and there's lots of little kids yelling and Grandma wants me to play with them 'cause she's tired. And then I'm too tired for homework!

Tory: My cousins are always rowdy and it's hard to concentrate.

Pause

Michael: I have Little League right after school and by the time we get home it's late.

Pause

Teacher: It sounds like some kids find it hard to concentrate after school, some don't have the help they need, and some have other things to do. What kinds of things might help kids get homework done when they're finding it hard to concentrate?

SUMMARY

Good listening is indispensable to teaching and is part of using good teacher language. Far from simply receiving students' words passively, to listen means to search for the speaker's intended meaning beneath the words. When teachers truly listen to students, students feel known, learn more about themselves, feel more like they belong to a community, and become better communicators. Listening also helps teachers ask better questions and inspires students to take their learning more seriously. Two technical strategies—pausing and paraphrasing—can make teachers better listeners. When we use these strategies with the true intention of understanding what and how our students think and feel, we elevate the quality of our teaching.

WORKS CITED

Fitzhenry, Robert I. 1987. *Barnes & Noble Book of Quotations.* New York: Barnes and Noble Books.

Garmston, Robert and Bruce M. Wellman. 1999. *The Adaptive School: A Sourcebook for Developing Collaborative Groups.* Norwood, MA: Christopher-Gordon Publishers, Inc.

CHAPTER FIVE

Reinforcing Language: Seeing Children and Naming Their Strengths

Children build on their strengths, not their weaknesses. This is one of the most important things to keep in mind when teaching. The implication for teacher language is that it's as important for us to see and name what children are doing well as to identify how they can improve. This is true whether we're teaching academic or social skills.

"I see lots of people remembering to push in their chairs before they line up," a teacher might say. Here are some other examples:

"Did you notice how many classmates shared thoughtful questions about the butterflies we observed? What a long list we have!"

"You were a big help when you translated the directions so Angela could understand them, Annie."

"In your story, the way you compared your feelings to a volcano about to explode is very powerful, Jeffrey. Did you realize that you used a simile there?"

These are all examples of reinforcing language, statements that identify and affirm students' specific positive actions. This kind of language is enormously powerful because it helps children recognize exactly what they're doing well and when they're on the right track. This allows them to grow further.

Yet reinforcing language is one of the most underused of teaching tools. One possible reason, an understandable one, is that with the day-to-day pressures of teaching, it can be easy for us to lose sight of what students are doing well or to take it for granted. In our desire to see students gain ground, we focus most of our attention on what they could improve. But it's important to remember the value of also looking for what they're doing well and reflecting that back to them. Children need to know their strengths in order to know what to stand on as they reach for the next higher rung. They need our words to help them do this.

Teachers often say that they do reinforce students' strengths when they tell students "Great job!" or "Well done!" However, there's a difference between giving those kinds of general praise and describing specific positives in the student's work or behavior. The latter is what's meant by "reinforcing language" in this book. (For more on the difference between these two ways of speaking, see the section "Praise and Reinforcing Language" later in this chapter.)

Before going into the details of using reinforcing language, it's important to pause and remember how critical it is for teachers to carefully observe their students. In order to see and mirror back to children their strengths and positive actions, we must first see children as the whole people that they are. My colleague Ruth Charney notes the importance of seeing "their interests, their sadnesses, their delights, the fact that they always bring their baseball cards to school, the fact that one day a child comes into the room with a bag under her arm and doesn't part with it." She continues, "This larger seeing of children, not just seeing whether they follow directions, know routines, or put details into their writing, is what allows teachers to use reinforcing language effectively." There are many practical ways to become more observant of children, ranging from circulating the room while children are working to walking at the back of the line when they're going down the hall. The important thing is that we do observe, for we have to see the entire child to see the child's true strengths.

When to Use Reinforcing Language

Teachers can use reinforcing language to great benefit in a variety of situations: to coach children on key behaviors as they practice social and academic skills, to help a group move past stuck points, to point out individual children's "leading edge" behaviors, and to make children more aware of their growth by describing "learning histories."

Coaching performance

We've all heard coaches and parents shouting encouragement to children as they practice sport skills. "That's just the way to angle your foot, Kim!" "Look at how you choked up on that bat, Jamie!" "You're running fast today, Iliana!"

Classrooms should be full of the same types of encouragement. "You were all lined up in one minute flat this time!" "Such careful writing you're doing." "Listen to all the different ideas you have about this!" A teacher can routinely watch for children practicing the skills they're working on and encourage them as they go. Just as good coaches use such encouraging language to help players improve on the field, good teachers use it to help students grow in the classroom.

Helping a group move past a stuck point

Children are bound to make mistakes and test limits in the areas that they're struggling with. But in the midst of all this, they're also likely to show bits of well-intentioned and skillful behavior. Teachers who observe students carefully in the midst of a chaotic transition, for example, will see that some children are following directions, helping each other, or remaining calm and task-oriented. Without ignoring misbehavior, we can support children's growth by noticing these positive behaviors and describing them specifically.

Mr. Parks's fourth grade class was one of the most impulsive and squirmy groups he had ever taught. Class discussions were continually interrupted by children speaking out of turn, talking to neighbors, or playing with small objects. Despite spending a lot of time making and discussing rules for group discussions, the class seemed to make little progress. Mr. Parks decided to try a different approach. During a typically unfocused discussion that nonetheless included a few examples of constructive behavior, he stopped and remarked, "You know, I've noticed that several children are sitting calmly and listening when others are speaking, and we're hearing some good ideas from people. What are some other things you've noticed that are going well in this discussion?"

The children sat up a little straighter and leaned forward in interest. "Lots of kids are raising their hands and not calling out," one student shared.

"I didn't fool around with my erasers. I just sat here," Mark announced.

"I noticed a couple of you even sat on your hands for a bit," Mr. Parks observed. "That's one way to keep your hands empty so you can concentrate. What else could you do to make our discussion even more focused and productive?"

Given this positive framing, the children were willing to share ideas for further improvement. They mentioned that they all could make sure their hands were empty, resist the urge to talk to their neighbors, and be more consistent in waiting for a turn to speak.

"Let's try these," Mr. Parks suggested. The group's subsequent behavior was not perfect, but it was better.

When children are struggling, reinforcing those aspects of their behavior that do demonstrate skill and good intention in the midst of the problems may provide them the motivation to improve. It reassures the children that they are on the path to success and that their efforts are noticed and valued.

Notice in the above example that Mr. Parks didn't say, "*I like* the way several children are sitting calmly … ," or "I've noticed that *Tim and Marissa* are sitting calmly …" These wordings, while they sound positive, can backfire. The first instance sends the message that the reason to behave positively is to please their teacher, and the second instance holds some children up as examples at the expense of others. (To learn more, see the sections "Emphasize description over personal approval" and "Avoid naming some individuals as examples for others" later in this chapter.)

POINTING OUT INDIVIDUAL CHILDREN'S LEADING EDGE BEHAVIORS

Related to helping a group move past a stuck point is alerting individual children of their leading edge behaviors. Peter Johnston defines the "leading edge" as "where the student has reached beyond herself, stretching what she knows just beyond its limit, producing something that is partly correct." (Johnston 2004, 13) Pointing out a child's leading edge can be very effective in supporting increasingly skillful behavior.

Ms. James noticed that Bria, who often speaks out impulsively without waiting her turn, today began to speak out, caught herself, and raised her hand and waited to be called on. "I notice you're remembering to raise your hand today," Ms. James told Bria privately later. "That helped our discussion include lots of different kids' ideas." Bria still forgot to raise her hand sometimes after that day, but the times when she did remember represented partial progress toward her goal and were therefore important moments for the teacher to affirm.

In the above example, it was important that Ms. James spoke to Bria individually after the group discussion. In general, it's best to point out children's leading edge behavior privately because doing so publicly may inadvertently also highlight their weaknesses to classmates. Because the teacher shared her observation privately, Bria was able to focus on how she had grown rather than on what her classmates might be thinking about her. Of course, if we're pointing out the leading edge behavior of the class as a whole, we'd speak to the whole class.

Describing learning histories

Pointing out children's "learning histories" (Johnston 2004, 14) involves comparing their current behavior to less skilled earlier behaviors. This builds a scaffold for children's growth by reminding students that learning is an ongoing process, not simply an end product.

"Yesterday it took you five minutes to get ready for library, and today it only took three. What allowed you to be ready more quickly?" we might say to a class.

A child struggling to learn to read may be encouraged when we ask, "Remember when you had trouble reading some of the words you read today with no trouble at all?"

A group of children rightfully feels proud and competent when we remind them, "A few weeks ago the list of things we know about rocks was one page long. Now we have three pages full of things you know about rocks."

Effective Reinforcing Language

Reinforcing language can be used to highlight a variety of student strengths: their skills, their attitudes, processes they used, or quality work they did. Here are some points to remember when using this kind of language:

* Name concrete, specific behaviors.

* Use a warm and professional tone.

* Emphasize description over personal approval.

* Consider adding a question to extend student thinking.

* Find positives to name in all students.

* Avoid naming individuals as examples for others.

NAME CONCRETE, SPECIFIC BEHAVIORS

Reinforcing language goes beyond a general response such as "Good job!", "Beautiful drawing!", or even "That shows good citizenship!" It's more concrete and specific, communicating exactly which aspects of students' behavior, products, or processes are working well or are steps in the right direction.

For example, observing a particularly productive math session, a teacher is struck by how focused the children are and how readily they're sharing their ideas with each other. At the end of the session, the teacher says, "You really concentrated on your math work today. I also saw lots of you sharing ideas about how to solve the problems with each other." If the teacher had noticed that the children were gaining mastery of large numbers, she might have said, "You're catching on to reading large numbers. Last week we worked with numbers up to one thousand, and today you read numbers up into the millions!"

Identifying and describing such behaviors helps children become more aware of what they know, what they can do, and how they have progressed. Such awareness of the desirable behaviors in their repertoire allows them to pull the behaviors up more easily and reuse, hone, and build on them—actions that lead the children to optimal growth and learning.

Does this mean teachers should never say "Good job" or "Beautiful work"? No. There is a place for such general praise. The key is to be clear on our purpose in giving feedback. When the purpose is to celebrate with children, general praise can do the job. But when our purpose is to instruct or foster change and growth, naming concrete, specific positives is more effective. (To learn more, see the section "Praise and Reinforcing Language" later in this chapter.)

When recognizing children's positive behaviors, we should name only those behaviors that actually occurred. This may sound obvious, but in an effort to maintain a supportive tone when children make mistakes or forget expectations, it's common for teachers to slip into naming behaviors that are hoped for but not yet achieved.

"I see children sitting quietly with their hands to themselves," I once heard a teacher say to her squirming, tussling group. Later, when several children spoke out of turn, she said, "Thank you for waiting for your turn to speak."

Although the intention is positive, such language, because it is indirect, can feel manipulative to children and can undermine their relationship with the teacher. A more effective way to guide students toward expected behaviors is to give them a reminder. (See Chapter 6 to learn about reminding language.)

EXAMPLES OF NAMING CONCRETE, SPECIFIC BEHAVIORS

Instead of:	Try:
"Your spelling shows progress."	"You remembered to change the 'y' to 'i' when adding 'ed.'"
"Terrific meeting today!"	"I noticed lots of careful listening and pausing to think before talking."
"Nice job with your note taking."	"I see you wrote the main ideas in your own words and carefully noted where you got the information."
"I noticed how hard you worked."	"You kept working on this a long time. And when you didn't know the answer right away, you tried a different strategy or asked someone for help."

USE A WARM AND PROFESSIONAL TONE

Many of us use words such as "sweetie" or "honey" when we address family members or friends. When we work in our professional role as teachers, however, such terms can undermine the professional teacher–student relationship.

My friend's son was getting bad reports about his behavior in English one year. When his mother asked him what was going on, he told her, "I can't stand my English teacher!" This was puzzling because the teacher had a fine reputation, and this child did not generally express aversion to teachers. When my friend went to observe the class one day though, she knew what the problem was: overly sentimental talk. The teacher opened the class by saying in a singsong, high-pitched voice, "Well, chickadees, look at how beautifully you prepared for our lesson!" She called on students with phrases such as "What do you think, darling?" and "Let's hear from you, honey." Often she put her hand on top of students' heads. My friend's son did not respond well to this kind of communication.

This teacher no doubt was trying to show affection for her students, but her language made this student feel more like a pet or infant than a competent and independent learner. When we use overly sentimental tones and touch, we risk patronizing children despite our best intentions. Children may resent—or live up to—the implicit expectation that they have limited capacities.

Our communication is more effective and powerful when we use a warm but professional tone. "I see you've all prepared beautifully for our lesson" conveys appreciation for the students' effort. "What do you think, Lin?" communicates respect for Lin's intelligence. Students on the receiving end of such language will feel assured that their teacher knows them as the intelligent, capable individuals that they are—and they will understand that their teacher likes them.

EMPHASIZE DESCRIPTION OVER PERSONAL APPROVAL

We're more likely to encourage skill growth and autonomy in children when we de-emphasize our personal approval and focus instead on clearly naming specific positives in the children. For example, a teacher might observe, "You took your time to check your work today before turning it in" instead of "I loved how you checked your work before turning it in." In place of "I like it when children line up so nicely," it's more effective to say "Did you notice how quickly and calmly you lined up today?"

When we focus on our feelings about children's behavior, we send an implicit message that the purpose of good behavior is to please us, when what we want is for children to be motivated toward cooperative, careful behaviors for the sake of themselves and the group. When we focus on our own feelings, we undermine the children's sense of self-control, intrinsic motivation, and authentic community.

"But how can I convey warmth and my true appreciation if I don't say 'I love that drawing'?" some teachers ask. The answer is that when we describe behaviors which we genuinely value and are important for children's growth and success, our warmth and caring will naturally come through in our tone of voice and body language. Emphasizing description over teacher approval does not mean pretending we have no feelings. Our appreciation is there when we say with genuine enthusiasm, "I'm hearing lots of friendly conversations and seeing people helping each other." But our feelings are not the central focus, as it is when we say, "I love how you're having friendly conversations and helping each other."

It's true that even if we make an effort to de-emphasize our personal approval, there are students who will habitually bring a piece of work to us and ask, "Do you like it?" How are we to respond?

I've found that the question "Do you like it?" is one way that some children have learned to extract praise from teachers. It's as though they're saying, "I crave your good opinion. Please tell me you like it!" It seems cruel not to give them the expected praise. But children who ask for such praise have been taught to let others do their thinking and judging for them. If we supply the praise, we're fueling that over-reliance on external validation.

An alternative way to respond is to carefully examine the work the child is showing and describe what we see. "Here's what I notice about this work," we might say, then name some interesting and skillful aspects we observed. We can then ask the child, "What do you like about your work?" or "What else would you like me to know about this work?"

If we don't have time for all of this in the moment, we can say, "Think about what you most like about this work, and I'll check back in later so you can show me."

Another approach is to teach children not to ask the question. With the class, we can generate ideas for what characterizes good work, post the ideas, and teach students to ask themselves, "How does my work compare with this list?" When they want feedback from others, instead of asking "Do you like it?" children can learn to ask questions such as "What's interesting about it?" "What do you notice about it?" and "Would you like to know what I like about it?"

Does this mean we should never tell children we like their work or are pleased with something they did? No. As with general praise such as "Great job," there are times when it's appropriate to give children our personal approval. It all depends on the goal of our communication at any given moment. (See "Praise and Reinforcing Language" later in this chapter to learn more.)

Related to using "I like how you …" or "I love the way you …" is the use of "Thank you" when trying to support children's positive behavior. We generally say "thank you" when people do us a favor. If a child runs an errand for me or helps me clean up a spill, it's completely appropriate for me to thank the child. But if I say "Thank you for listening" when listening is essential to participating constructively in an activity, I'm implying that the child is listening in order to help me, and not for the sake of his or her own learning. If I say "Thank you for lining up so quickly," I can actually undermine students' sense of self-control because I'm showing that I believe they're lining up quickly to please me, not to become ever less dependent of my oversight. It's more effective to simply say "You listened carefully to the others in the circle" and "You lined up so quickly this time!"

EXAMPLES OF EMPHASIZING DESCRIPTION
OVER PERSONAL APPROVAL

Instead of:	Try:
"I'm so pleased with the way you all helped each other with cleanup so you could finish faster."	"You all helped each other with cleanup so you could finish faster."
"Thank you for your thoughtful suggestions to the younger students."	"You gave thoughtful suggestions to the younger students. I'm sure they found them helpful."

Instead of:	Try:
"I love how quiet the room was and how busily everyone was working."	"Did you notice how quiet the room was and how busily everyone was working?"

CONSIDER ADDING A QUESTION TO EXTEND STUDENT THINKING

To extend students' thinking, we can follow statements about their positive behaviors with an open-ended question. The goal of the question might be to help students become more aware of the behaviors named, to deepen their understanding of how such behavior is helpful, or to help them see what they can do to improve further. After observing, "You've been concentrating hard on your reading, Jem," I might ask, "What's helping you concentrate so well today?" The point of this question is to help Jem become aware of successful strategies that may help him further strengthen his ability to concentrate during class.

If, alternatively, my purpose is to help Jem realize which aspects of reading hold allure for him, I might ask, "What about that chapter is interesting to you?"

To a student experimenting with multicolored artwork, I might say, "You're using a lot of colors in that picture," and then add, "How do you like the way it's turning out?" By prompting the student to relate process to product, I help him understand how using a lot of colors can be desirable for a certain effect.

"You finished your work with plenty of time to spare today," a teacher might say to a class. "How does that feel?" This can help students become aware that they're feeling calm, successful, perhaps glad to have time to look back at their work, and maybe interested in doing more because they have time to think about what they could add. This awareness helps solidify for students that it's a good idea to stay focused in order to get their work done efficiently. (To learn more about open-ended questions, see Chapter 3.)

Find positives to name in all students

Reinforcing language can and should be used with all students, not just those who are "best." Even when children's behavior or work isn't where we want it to be, we can see some positive aspects and perhaps some growth if we observe carefully. Edward is still not writing more than a couple of sentences to accompany his drawings, but his teacher did notice that he spent more time today on the writing than the drawing. She says to him, "You seem to have put extra effort into your writing today, Edward." On the playground, Vivian often bossed and intimidated her classmates. Sitting down to discuss this with her, the teacher began by observing, "Vivian, I noticed you have a lot of ideas for how to play games during recess." This affirmed a strength of Vivian's and provided a positive foundation for the rest of the discussion.

It's important not to confuse this encouraging approach with showering children with positive feedback every time they do any small thing right. We should be selective, describing only those behaviors that are truly important and relevant to a child's growth or a group's shared goals. The same behavior may pass this test for one child but not another; it depends on what competencies or habits the child is working on. For example, using a sharp pencil to do work may be a small enough deal for most students that it doesn't warrant a teacher comment. But if a certain student habitually uses dull pencils, producing smudgy, illegible work, and is working on remembering to sharpen his pencil, then it would be meaningful for the teacher to say to him, "I noticed you sharpened your pencil first today." As teachers, we know the areas of growth that are important for students to work on currently. Our job is to notice when students make progress in those areas and reinforce those behaviors.

Naming positives in all children also does not mean that we have to do this equally with all children at every moment. Those who are off task should be reminded or have their behavior redirected, not reinforced. It does mean that over time, we see accomplishments, growth, and leading edge behaviors in all students, and we name them.

AVOID NAMING SOME INDIVIDUALS AS
EXAMPLES FOR OTHERS

"See how neat Ronna's handwriting is?" a teacher says to a class, with the intention of encouraging them to make their writing neater—more like Ronna's. "I like the way Hugo and Marlee have looked through three sources for their research projects. Let's see how many others can do that as well," another teacher says.

Such language may sound encouraging at first because it names positive things that Ronna, Hugo, and Marlee did. In actuality, it can be extremely damaging because it makes or implies comparisons among children, elevating some at the expense of others. All who are not lauded have been, by implication, devalued or criticized. If we want students to write neatly or to look through three sources for their research projects, we should simply say exactly that, without naming any individuals, and perhaps prompt students to plan how they will accomplish those goals. For example: "Your task is to look through three sources. What can help you find three appropriate sources?"

A more subtle but still problematic version of elevating some children at the expense of others is to set up a competition among the class. Early in my career, for example, I learned I could handle transition times by saying, "I'm looking to see which table is quietest" or "Let's see who can be ready first." Although this often got the behavior I wanted, it did so at a price: The children who were first or quietest or neatest got to feel triumphant, but the others felt unimportant or even dejected. I could have said "I see more and more children sitting quietly. I see some other children really working on putting things away so they can be ready soon." Such language does not compare the children to each other, but simply takes note of positive steps in the process of making a transition.

EXAMPLES OF ENCOURAGING WITHOUT
ELEVATING INDIVIDUALS

Instead of:	Try:
"I like the way Reid and Tran followed the directions. Who else?"	"I see some names on the sign-up board. Who can remind us of the sign-up procedure?"
"Notice how Liselle put her backpack and coat in the cubby so they both fit? Let's see if everyone can do that."	"I notice that all the backpacks and coats are in the general cubby area. What else could we do to make that area even neater?"
"Let's see which table can get their supplies together the fastest."	"I see lots of supplies being gathered. We'll begin when every table is ready."
"Yesterday, Group 1 took twelve seconds to move their chairs into the circle. Let's see if you all can do it just as quickly."	"Yesterday, you all cut two seconds off your chair-moving time. Let's see if we can set a class record today."

PRAISE AND REINFORCING LANGUAGE

What about giving children general praise such as "Good job!" or "Super!"? Isn't it a good thing for students to get this type of praise from their teachers? Sometimes. It depends on the purpose. Is such praise intended to bring us more control over children, or to allow us to celebrate with them?

PRAISE USED FOR CONTROL

Sometimes teachers praise children with phrases like those above so that children will keep doing the positive things that earned the praise. For example, after a child works hard on an outline for a report, we say "Good job!" or "I like the way you worked!" with the hope that this will encourage the child to keep working hard on future assignments. Our intention is good and the method seems sensible. But research indicates that if our purpose is to influence children's behavior, general praise that emphasizes teacher approval is actually counterproductive. Using praise this way decreases students' intrinsic motivation and true self-esteem. (Deci and Flaste 1995) It makes students rely too much on pleasing the teacher and too little on their own desire to learn, grow, and be a contributing member of a community. Their self-control, initiative, creativity, and sense of personal responsibility are ultimately undermined. (Chandler 1981; Green and Lepper 1974; Martin 1977; Stringer and Hurt 1981)

This kind of general teacher praise that aims to influence behavior, which Edward Deci calls "controlling praise" (Deci and Flaste 1995, 68), can be even more problematic when it focuses on final products rather than processes. While final products are important, it can be damaging to overemphasize them at the expense of paying attention to the way students work and their incremental successes along the way. "That's A+ work!" a teacher praises when a child answers all the questions on an assignment correctly. But what about the student who has come up with inventive strategies or shown great persistence in finding answers that are not 100 percent correct? What general praise can we give to that student? "Good try"? The implication is that this student's effort, though commendable, was ultimately lacking. When the best praise is reserved for the child who produces a perfect final product, any other praise is, by comparison, discouraging.

The kind of reinforcing language discussed in this book is different from controlling praise (though both are intended to influence behavior), because reinforcing language puts the focus on children's specific actions. It draws children's attention to their own creativity, attention to detail, or other strength, rather than the teacher's judgment. It therefore fosters children's sense of autonomy and competence.

PRAISE USED FOR CELEBRATION

There are times when our purpose in praising students is not to affect their behavior, but simply to express delight, one human being to another. Reading a piece of fiction a student wrote, a teacher is genuinely tickled by the conclusion. "I love the way you ended your story!" she exclaims spontaneously. She doesn't say this to get the student to keep writing good conclusions or to teach the student anything. Rather, she's expressing true personal appreciation.

In such cases, general praise can be appropriate. A sincere "Good idea!" or "What a beautiful drawing!" can build genuinely warm and mutually respectful relationships between teachers and students. It's an important way to build a positive classroom climate. The tone of such praise is spontaneous and warm, and we don't expect anything from our students in return. We're saying "I'm enjoying you just the way you are."

Admittedly, in everyday classroom life, it can be hard in the moment to know whether some praise we're about to give is controlling or celebratory in intention. Distinguishing the often subtle difference between the two requires that we be honest with ourselves. If we hold any expectation that our praise will influence a child's subsequent behavior in any way, we have crossed the line into controlling praise. When in doubt, it's better to give specific, descriptive feedback, which we can always count on to be supportive of children's learning.

Another thing to remember is that it's fine to use genuinely celebratory praise as long as it does not replace or reduce our use of reinforcing language. As my colleague Marlynn Clayton points out, our primary job is to teach respectfully, not to be a friend to our students. It's the reinforcing language that helps us do our job. Teachers therefore should strive for a balance and tip toward more use of reinforcing language. Sometimes the two kinds of language may even be combined. I recently heard a teacher respond to a student's writing with, "Oh, lovely work! You described that character's feelings with such detail that she came alive for me."

Finally, if we use celebratory praise, it's critical that we find genuine reasons to use it with all students equally. This means that, as with the use of reinforcing language, we make a habit of observing children carefully, so that we see and hear things that we truly enjoy and appreciate about each of them.

REINFORCING LANGUAGE IN ACTION

Reinforcing language can be used in all situations throughout a school day, from arrival to dismissal, during group activities and independent work. Here are examples:

DURING TRANSITIONS

"I see trash going into trash cans. I see backpacks put away."

"Lots of you are playing the quiet hand game we learned to help us through waiting time."

"You got to the rug for dismissal in forty-seven seconds. That's a record!"

"Yesterday it took eight minutes for everyone to settle down with a book after recess. Today it only took five. What caused the difference?"

"I noticed that when I gave the three minute warning, lots of you started wrapping up and putting your folders in the bin."

DURING GROUP ACTIVITIES

"Did you notice how many facts we listed about vernal pools? This class knows a lot about that topic!"

"Listen to the respectful words you're using!"

"I noticed people giving supportive clues. What are some other things you noticed that made this activity go well?"

"You brought clipboards and pencils. That's one way to remember the ideas from this discussion."

"A few weeks ago we had only one street and four buildings in our model town. Now we have many streets and nearly twenty-five buildings."

DURING INDEPENDENT WORK TIME

"You used several sound words in this poem. It helps the reader 'hear' what you're describing."

"Lots of good interview questions being jotted down."

"I see you're checking your work before turning it in."

"You decided to use different colors this time. What was your thinking there?"

"Many of you are remembering to put the books back in their original bins so others can find them."

"Oh, I see you're using chapter headings in your writing. You seem to be picking up something from the books you're reading."

"So many problems done! You're getting fast with multiplication."

IN ONE-ON-ONE CONVERSATIONS

"You showed kindness during recess yesterday when you asked Didi to join the game."

"I notice you're speaking more loudly in discussions. That helps us know your ideas."

"Remember when you thought fractions were really hard? Today you did all the fractions problems with no trouble."

"You and Tamika exchanged some good ideas today. What made that go so well?"

"You've been taking risks in the skits by accepting harder roles. How does that feel?"

"I notice you stayed quieter today so your tablemates could talk more."

SUMMARY

Reinforcing language names for students what they're doing well, whether in the social or academic realm. This kind of language is vitally important in helping children grow because children build on their strengths, not their weaknesses. Reinforcing language can be used throughout the school day for a variety of purposes: to let students know what behaviors are valued, to encourage students as they stretch themselves, to help them get past some point they're stuck on, and to compare their current and past skill levels to help them see that learning is a process. In all these cases, we're most effective if we name specific behaviors, emphasize description over teacher approval, use a warm and professional tone, and name only those behaviors and skills that are truly important for students to work on currently. It's important to use this kind of encouraging language with all students, not just those who are "good" or "best," for if we observe carefully enough, we will see all children taking noteworthy steps in their growth.

WORKS CITED

Chandler, T.A. 1981. "What's Wrong with Success and Praise?" *Arithmetic Teacher* 29(4): 1–12.

Deci, Edward L. and Richard Flaste. 1995. *Why We Do What We Do: Understanding Self-Motivation*. New York: Penguin Books.

Green, D. and M. R. Lepper. 1974. "How to Turn Play into Work." *Psychology Today* 8(4): 49–54.

Johnston, Peter H. 2004. *Choice Words*. Portland, ME: Stenhouse Publishers.

Martin, D.L. 1977. "Your Praise Can Smother Learning." *Learning* 5(6): 43–51.

Stringer, B.R. and H.T. Hurt. 1981. "To Praise or Not to Praise: Factors to Consider Before Utilizing Praise as a Reinforcing Device in the Classroom Communication Process." Paper presented at the annual meeting of the Southern Speech Communications Association, Austin, TX. April 8–10.

CHAPTER SIX

Reminding Language:
Helping Students Remember
Expectations

Few of us can get through a week or even a day without reminders, either giving them or getting them. "Remember to pick up the dry cleaning," I tell my husband as I head out the door. "Don't forget to call the repair man," he reminds me on another morning. "Don't forget your homework," I was urged as a child. "Remind me to … ," we often say to each other, or even "Remind me to remind you to …"

Just as reminders keep us organized and on track in our daily lives, they offer valuable support to students as they go about their busy classroom life:

"What are some things you can do today to keep recess safe and friendly for everyone?" Mr. Kowalski asks his class as they wait in line before going outside.

In another classroom, Evangeline wanders over to speak to a friend during silent reading time. "Evangeline, what are you supposed to be doing right now?" Ms. Adamson asks her.

In Mr. Griffon's room, the students are nearing the end of a project time. "In a few minutes it will be time to clean up," he announces. "What might you begin to do now so you will be ready?"

Although reminders in the classroom share similarities with reminders in everyday life, there is one crucial difference. Usually when we give reminders in everyday life, we tell our listener what it is they should remember. In the opening examples of this chapter, the reminder tells the listener to pick up the dry cleaning, to call the repair man, to bring the homework.

By contrast, the classroom reminders discussed in this chapter prompt children to do the remembering themselves. All three teachers in the above examples refrain from naming the desired behavior. Instead, they tell the children to pull up their memory of established expectations—for having a safe and friendly recess, for behavior during quiet reading time, and for how to prepare for cleanup—and then allow the children to decide on an action based on those expectations. Reminding language supports children in pausing and visualizing what to do before they take action.

Used in this way, reminding language helps children develop the feelings of autonomy and competence that lead to self-control and intrinsic motivation. We communicate an assumption that students are competent learners and have good intentions, even when their behavior is beginning to go off track. In classrooms where the use of reminding language is the norm, the children develop habits of attending carefully to expectations because they know they will truly be expected to remember them and behave accordingly.

EFFECTIVE REMINDING LANGUAGE

Reminders are useful in a wide range of classroom situations, from transitions to whole group discussions. Whatever the situation, these guidelines can make classroom reminders more effective:

* Start by establishing expectations clearly.

* Phrase a reminder as a question or a statement.

* Use a direct tone and neutral body language.

* Use reminders proactively or reactively.

* Use reminders when the child and you are both calm.

* Keep reminders brief.

* Watch for follow-through.

START BY ESTABLISHING EXPECTATIONS CLEARLY

Children can only be reminded of what they already know. For reminding language to be successful, then, teachers first need to take the time to establish and teach expectations for children's behavior. A good way to do this is to hold structured discussions about the expectations, then follow with interactive modeling and practice.

Structured discussions

The goal of discussing an expectation is to help children connect it with specific behaviors. "Our rules say that we will respect each other. What if someone is sharing work with the class? What will we be doing if we are being respectful of the sharer?" Ms. Barnes asks the class. She's deliberate in saying the words "respect each other" and "being respectful of the sharer." Explicitly naming the goal is an important part of teaching expectations.

"We would look at the person who is sharing and not talk to each other," says Lily.

"We probably shouldn't make faces or act like we don't like the sharing," Ben adds.

"If we're not making faces, what can we do instead?" Ms. Barnes asks.

"Just a normal face," Ben responds, and others nod.

"Sure. You could also have an interested expression," Ms. Barnes says. "What might an interested expression look like? Who wants to show us?"

So went a typical structured discussion about showing respect. Notice that the children are invited to think about and name the positive behaviors that will help them meet expectations. Being actively involved in this way helps children truly internalize the expectations.

Occasionally we want to teach behaviors that children have little knowledge of. In that case, a discussion in which we ask them to think about and share their prior experiences with the behavior wouldn't be very fruitful. In those situations teachers might therefore skip the structured discussion and go to interactive modeling. For example, kindergartners about to go to their first school-wide assembly would have little sense of what to expect at such a gathering. To help them prepare, I would begin with a modeling session that shows the safe and considerate behavior expected of them.

Interactive modeling

Interactive modeling includes the teacher modeling a desired behavior, but also extends beyond that. It actively involves the children in naming what the modeled behaviors are, and then in practicing the behaviors themselves while the teacher watches and provides feedback.

Let's continue with the example of Ms. Barnes teaching the class how to be a respectful audience member when someone shares. "I'm going to show what it looks like when I'm listening to someone share," she says as she begins the modeling phase of the lesson. "We need a volunteer to pretend to be sharing work." She calls on Terry, who stands and pretends to hold up a sheet of paper. Ms. Barnes says, "Okay, I'm going to be respectful to Terry. See what you notice." The teacher again deliberately names that she is going to be "respectful." This strengthens for children the connection between the goal and the modeled behaviors.

Ms. Barnes sits with her hands quietly resting in her lap and her feet on the floor. She looks directly at Terry's imaginary paper with a serious expression. She smiles for a moment, then raises her hand. Before Terry can pretend to call on her, she lowers her hand and says, "Okay, stop. Thank you, Terry." Turning to the class, she asks, "What did I do that was respectful?"

The children name several things: she held her hands and feet still, her hands were empty, her face showed attention and interest. "And you raised your hand like you had a question or comment for me," Terry adds.

Modeling is crucial because in addition to talking about expectations, children need to see examples of expected behaviors. After they see, it's important that they name what they saw. It is this naming that allows children to truly grasp what the expected behaviors are. It's what makes modeling powerful.

Practice

After modeling comes practice, when students try out the behaviors that were just modeled and named. It would be folly simply to model and then assume that everybody will know exactly what to do. Children, even older children, need opportunities to try the behaviors themselves in supervised, low-stakes circumstances. Their teacher and classmates can then immediately reinforce what they did well, and the student can quickly correct mistakes. Only after this practice can we assume that students are prepared to consistently behave in the expected ways in the course of classroom life.

"Now we're going to pretend again," Ms. Barnes tells the group. "We need a new volunteer to pretend to be the sharer and a couple of volunteers to show us respectful listening."

Hands wave and the teacher selects a sharer and two listeners who she expects will model the positive behaviors she has just demonstrated.

"Watch carefully to see how many ways Dan and Eva show us that they are respectful listeners." As in the discussion and modeling steps, she explicitly ties the goal of being "respectful" with the behaviors the class is about to see.

After Dan and Eva model and the children describe how they showed respect, Ms. Barnes takes a final step. "This time, I'm going to pretend that I'm the sharer, and all of you will show respectful listening."

She stands and holds up a book as though she is reading aloud from it. The children sit calmly and focus their attention on her. After a few moments, Ms. Barnes closes the book.

"I know I really felt respected!" she tells them. "What were you doing that helped me feel that way?" Once again the children are guided to do the crucial step of naming the positive behaviors they saw.

In this example, the practice was done in two parts: First, a few students practiced while the rest of the class observed, then the whole class practiced. In older grades, teachers might skip the first step and go directly to whole-class practice.

After this kind of formal, structured practice, many teachers deliberately cue students to put the behaviors into action during real classroom work while they observe and coach. For example, when Ms. Barnes's class finishes the formal practice above, she says, "After lunch you'll be sharing your wetlands reports. You'll have another chance to practice respectful behavior." Then, right before the actual sharing, Ms. Barnes reminds the group, "Think about how you will be a respectful listener." She herself prepares to focus not only on the students' sharing, but on how well the class uses the respectful listening behaviors they just practiced. During the session, she quietly issues reminders and redirections to students who need them, and at the end of the session she reinforces the respectful behaviors she observed in the group.

PHRASE A REMINDER AS A QUESTION OR A STATEMENT

Reminders in the form of a question

One great way to give a reminder is to phrase it as a question: "What are you supposed to be doing right now?" "What should you be doing next?" "What can you do to solve that problem?" "When do we get lunches out?" Such questions directly prompt children to think about what they know.

Not all questions make effective reminders, however. The above examples are successful because they're neutral in wording. Importantly, too, they work only if the teacher uses a neutral tone. Compare them with a question such as "What would you be doing now if you had listened to directions, Jeremy?" While this question may sound like a reminder, it actually has the effect of an accusation because it presupposes that Jeremy didn't listen. The question would be even more damaging if the teacher uses an exasperated or angry tone. In reality, Jeremy might have listened but then forgotten the directions in the moment. Even if Jeremy truly did not listen, confronting him with that mistake is not the goal of reminders. Rather than communicate faith that he can meet behavior expectations, a question like this communicates distrust.

Another question that can communicate distrust is, "Why don't you [think about how you'll share beforehand, figure out how you'll clean up, etc.]." The phrase "Why don't you" carries a tone of recrimination, as if we're asking students to think about some wrong they committed and how they will now, finally, do it right.

We can keep our reminder questions neutral by maintaining our belief that children can and will do well, and then simply asking how they will achieve the positive goal: "What do the directions say to do now, Jeremy?" instead of "What would you be doing now if you had listened to directions, Jeremy?" "How will you clean up?" instead of "Why don't you figure out how you'll clean up?"

Reminders in the form of a statement

Reminders may also come in the form of statements that communicate the belief that children know what is expected of them. "I'll begin when everyone is ready." "I'm waiting for you to remember the rules." "Let's see if everyone can be in line and ready to go by the time I count to ten."

Another approach is to cue children with just a few words, not even a sentence. To a group that is interrupting each other in a discussion, I might say "Meeting rules," with no further explanation, and then wait for the group to become quiet and raise their hands. If children are off task during a cleanup, I might use a signal to get their attention, then simply say "Cleanup time."

Reminders sometimes take the form of directions that begin with "Show me …" or "Think about …": "Show me how you will move the chairs safely." "Show me how you use the calculator to check your work." "Think about where you will sit so you can do your best work." "Think about what will help you concentrate."

USE A DIRECT TONE AND NEUTRAL BODY LANGUAGE

Tone and body language are critical to the effectiveness of reminders. When we use a direct, open tone and keep our body language neutral, we communicate calmness and faith that children want to and are capable of being responsible, caring members of the class. Students are likely to take these kinds of reminders as honest, helpful prompts. If, on the other hand, we let our tone slide or our body language get sloppy, we risk communicating sarcasm, teasing, or other negative innuendos that embarrass or defeat our students.

For example, if I ask Mark "How do we use the paints?" with an even voice, a direct gaze, and a neutral body position, Mark very likely would immediately think about what we've established about using paints. But if I say the same words in a singsong voice, with arms crossed and eyes rolling, my message becomes an insult. Even if I'm trying to be humorous, I'm also implying that Mark is stupid. Rather than thinking about how to use paints, Mark is likely to be thinking about how I've just embarrassed him and possibly worrying that I don't like him.

Teachers are most likely to slip into sarcastic or teasing tones when we're feeling exasperated, angry, or tired. I know that when I'm feeling this way, I'm quite capable of using off-putting voices and body language. I know that to avoid this mistake, I have to manage my own emotions. And if my hold on my emotions is tenuous at the moment,

I'm best off trying an approach other than the use of reminders. (See the section "When Teachers Get Angry" later in this chapter.)

USE REMINDERS PROACTIVELY OR REACTIVELY

Reminding language may be used proactively to help children mentally rehearse appropriate behaviors before an activity or event, or it may be used reactively to support children in correcting themselves when their behavior is beginning to go off track.

Proactive reminders

Proactive reminders require teachers to think ahead about upcoming activities and predict aspects that will be challenging for students. While planning a science activity, Ms. Sauer thought about the possible difficulties the students might have and determined that working collaboratively was likely to be the most challenging for them. When introducing the activity to the class, she therefore said, "You're going to work in pairs to create a plan for testing the strength of these materials. What are some things you can do so both partners' ideas are included?" This served as an effective reminder of what the students had been learning and practicing about respectful partner work.

Another teacher in the same situation might decide that his students are most likely to struggle with using materials safely. He would then ask, "What are some things you can do to take care of all these materials and each other?" Or he might make the statement, "Think about how you will care for the materials and each other."

Proactive reminders generally work best if we name the positive expectation when giving the reminder. In the first example above, the teacher named the expectation that "both partners' ideas are included." In the second example, the teacher named the expectation that students would "take care of all these materials and each other."

Reactive reminders

Reactive reminders are reminders given after, or in reaction to, some student action. They're just as important and helpful to students as proactive reminders. Reactive reminders are most effective when they are used just as behavior is beginning to go off track, before the behavior is well under way or well established. This means teachers have to observe closely enough to notice small mistakes before they get big.

For example, while walking in line on the way to music, Mateo and Andrew begin poking each other. Ms. Dennis spots them and immediately says, "Mateo and Andrew, show me how to follow the rules in the halls." The two students stop their poking and resume walking with their hands to themselves.

To ask a child who is well along or deeply invested in a particular behavior to stop and think about expectations is not realistic and potentially counterproductive. In those cases, redirecting language would be more effective. (To learn about redirecting language, see Chapter 7.)

USE REMINDERS WHEN THE CHILD
AND YOU ARE BOTH CALM

Reminders are most effective when both the teacher and student are feeling calm. The teacher needs to be calm to give a reminder in a direct and trusting tone of voice. The student needs to be calm to think what the appropriate behavior is and act accordingly. This is why reminders should be used just as students are veering off course. Usually by the time misbehavior has gone on for a while, frustration is high and tempers are hot.

Picture, for example, what the example of Mateo and Andrew would have looked like if the teacher had waited to issue a reminder: After a few pokes back and forth, Mateo whispers "Stop it!" fiercely to Andrew while poking him on the arm. "You stop it!" Andrew whispers back, and escalates the exchange by poking Mateo in the chest. "You'd better stop or else!" Mateo says angrily, well above a whisper, then elbows Andrew's back. Within seconds the students are fighting. At this point Ms. Dennis strides up and says, "Boys, show me how you will follow the rules in the halls." They ignore her.

Ms. Dennis waited too long to try to reason with Mateo and Andrew. By this point both students were angry, out of control, and in no state of mind to think about hallway rules. What they needed now was to be firmly separated and taken to a place where they could calm down and regain their ability to reason.

Teachers, too, need to be calm for reminders to work. In this example, Ms. Dennis was relatively calm. But she could easily have been as angry as the students and just as unable to think and act rationally. Mateo and Andrew might have a pattern of fighting with each other. This might be the third time that day the teacher had to deal with their behavior. Ms. Dennis could be having an especially hard week. Any number of things could have sent her over the edge. Whatever the case, if she's angry, trying to use reminding language is likely to backfire because her tone is likely to be sharp and scolding. Everything about her words and affect is likely to convey that she does not believe the students want to and can behave responsibly. At such times, teachers need strategies beyond reminders. (See the section "When Teachers Get Angry" later in this chapter.)

KEEP REMINDERS BRIEF

As with all teacher language, the fewer words we use, the better. Usually the teacher says one or two short sentences at most. Our brevity gives students time and space to respond with their words and actions. I may be tempted to explain and reason, "Jana, we just went over what materials you need, and now you're not following directions. What materials should you be collecting?" Jana may feel fussed at, and the irritation may keep her from thinking clearly. Or she may simply lose the central message amidst all the words. It would've been better if I just said "Jana, what materials should you be collecting?"

EXAMPLES OF BRIEF REMINDERS

Instead of:	Try:
"We're going to join other classes in a few minutes for all-school meeting. We've talked about how we can be in control of ourselves when we're with other classes, and we've practiced. I want to see all of you remember what we learned. Who remembers how we show self-control?"	"We'll be going to all-school meeting in a few minutes. How will we show self-control?"
"Mia, you look like you're stuck on this problem. When you're stuck, are you supposed to make noises that distract others? Do you remember what we said about what to do when you're stuck?"	"Mia, what can you do if you get stuck on a problem?"
"Austin, you're going to hurt someone flinging the stick like that! Didn't we go over this? Were you listening?"	"Austin, safety rules."
"Before we start this meeting, I want everyone to think about being considerate and respectful in meetings because last week our meetings could've gone better. We have to do better this week."	"Before we start the meeting, let's review. What will help us have a good meeting?"

WATCH FOR FOLLOW-THROUGH

After giving a reminder, watch to make sure that children act. Did they indeed use friendly words during the group working session? The child who was about to snatch the markers and was given a reminder—did she then share the markers with her tablemates? If we don't watch for and require follow-through, children will learn to devalue reminders, and our language will lose its power. And what if children don't follow through? Then it's time for more directive language (see Chapter 7) or a logical consequence (see Brady et al. 2003 and Charney 2002).

Once children do correct their behavior after a reminder, we can acknowledge it with eye contact, a smile, a nod, or a wink. No words are necessary. Sometimes teachers say "Thank you" or praise children for correcting their behavior. But thanking the children implies that they corrected their behavior for our benefit, not their own. Similarly, praise used under these circumstances runs the risk of emphasizing teacher approval. (See the discussion of praise in Chapter 5.) Both undermine the goal of reminding language—to support children's sense of autonomy and competence.

STUDENTS WHO NEED REPEATED REMINDERS

Gina, with rare exception, jumps in with an answer when the teacher directs the question to someone else in the class. Nathan habitually rolls his eyes at classmates' comments during group discussions. We all have students who need frequent reminders about the same behaviors. If you're facing a situation like this, what can you do?

First, make sure you've carefully taught the expected behaviors to the class. Then try to find out why this particular student needs reminders over and over. Is there a particular reason the student has difficulty? To find out, take time to observe the child. Look for patterns. Does the student most need reminding during certain types of lessons or during less structured times, such as transitions?

After identifying patterns and triggers, look for a solution. If the child routinely misbehaves around a certain other student, keep the children apart for awhile. If the student tends to have trouble during certain instructional times, extra academic or social support can make all the difference. Often the support can be as simple as a brief private check-in at the beginning of a work period. Or it can be a small signal that the teacher and student agree on ahead of time. The teacher touching her ear, for example, might mean "What did we say about wait time?" or "Remember our rule about disagreeing respectfully." The teacher can then calmly make this signal to the student as needed without interrupting the discussion or lesson at hand.

Remember, too, to consider adjusting classroom routines for individual children if needed. For example, some children have a greater need to be active. For a child like this, the expectation may be to stay in Morning Meeting for the first fifteen minutes (and be just as attentive and focused as everyone else), but then to go help the custodian or do an errand for the teacher.

Another strategy is to arrange an individual conference with the child. Share your observations of the child's difficulties in meeting expectations, and ask the child for ideas about what might be causing the difficulties. You can also share a few theories of your own. Together, come up with some possible solutions and agree on one to try.

Once you feel sure that the expectations for a child's behavior are reasonable and the child has adequate support to meet those expectations, use logical consequences with consistency when the child doesn't follow through after a reminder.

One thing to avoid doing when the same child needs repeat reminders is to repeatedly issue reminders to the whole class, intending for the one child to hear and heed it. Chances are the child won't. Meanwhile, the public reminders may create resentment in the class toward the child who's having trouble.

(For more on individual conferences, see Charney 2004 or read about Social Conferences in Charney 2002. For more about logical consequences, see Brady et al. 2003.)

WHEN TEACHERS GET ANGRY

It's impossible to use reminders effectively when we're angry. But let's face it. We get angry sometimes. Teachers work hard. We put in long, sometimes stressful days, and despite our best efforts children will sometimes behave in ways that challenge and frustrate us. Anger is a natural reaction. And when we're really angry, our language usually shows it.

I admit that sometimes when I'm angry, words—often accusatory and hurtful—flow from my mouth with a life of their own. Although these words may temporarily stop misbehavior, they do so through intimidation and shaming. They teach children to either comply with or rebel against my will rather than teaching them self-control. So what do we do about anger?

The goal for teachers is not to avoid feeling angry, but to deal with our anger in ways that don't undermine respectful and trusting relationships with students. The challenge is to become aware of our anger just as we begin to feel it so that the emotion does not hijack our reason and good intentions. If our anger has escalated, the challenge then is to get through the moment keeping everyone as emotionally safe as possible.

Here are some tips:

PAY ATTENTION TO SMALL THINGS

The class is in the midst of a lesson and feeling pressured to meet a deadline. I see a group beginning to get edgy with each other. One student rolls her eyes at a classmate; another teases a neighbor. I'm tempted to ignore these little problems, hoping they'll go away while I attend to other things. But I know all too well from experience that often the bigger problems grow from these "small things." The eye rolls lead to an outright argument; the teasing becomes a shoving match. I know that as the small behaviors grow to big behaviors that I cannot ignore, my frustration will slowly escalate until I feel angry. So, I stop and say to the eye-roller, "Liz, respectful listening," and to the teaser, "Dominic, remember, friendly words." Reminding language works when problems are still small and the teacher is still calm.

USE A BRIEF PHRASE TO STOP THE ACTION

In the heat of frustration or anger, the teacher can buy some time to cool off by using a short stock phrase such as "Freeze!" or "Stop now!" This stops children's action long enough for teachers to collect their thoughts and continue with a reminder or a redirection in a matter-of-fact voice.

It was the end of a long day and Martin was challenging his tired teacher yet again. "Why do *I* have to clean up? I didn't make that mess!" he whined as he threw a wad of paper across the room. After a day of working hard to maintain her patience, the teacher immediately felt so frustrated and angry with Martin that her hands clenched into fists. "Stop now, Martin!" she said in a tight voice. Martin dropped his hands to his sides and turned to look at her with big eyes. The teacher allowed a moment of silence while she breathed, rehearsed what to say next, and brought her voice under control. "You have a job to do. You can do it now or you can sit here until you are ready to do it," she said firmly but more calmly. Martin sat.

Before using a stock phrase such as "Freeze!" or "Stop now!" it's important to teach children what to do when they hear it. This includes having them practice those responses before you need to use the phrases in a real situation.

USE TIME-OUT

Sometimes we need more than a momentary pause to collect ourselves, or the children might need a clearer break from the action before they are ready to regain self-control. At these times, a positive time-out can be a lifesaver. (See Brady et al. 2003 for more on the use of positive time-outs.) While the purpose of time-out is usually to allow children to collect themselves, it can also be used when teachers need some time to cool down and regroup.

Alicia, a student who seemed continually to seek conflict with her classmates, marched up to Ron and pushed him out of line. "That's my place!" she shouted. Her teacher was exasperated. "There she goes again. I've had it!" she thought angrily. Controlling her tone of voice, however, the teacher said evenly, "Alicia, take a break."

Because this teacher had taught all the children what to do when she told them "Take a break" (another way of saying "Take a time-out"), and had given them opportunities to practice, Alicia walked to the time-out chair with only a little huffiness, and sat. The teacher was then able to focus on the other children for awhile and regain her equanimity. She also had time to plan what she would say to Alicia when Alicia returned to the group.

GET HELP FROM ANOTHER TEACHER

Sometimes a child will not or cannot stop a behavior despite a time-out. A "buddy teacher time-out" can be very helpful in these situations. In a buddy teacher time-out, a colleague who's not emotionally involved in the situation comes and takes the child to another room, where the child takes a time-out under a watchful adult eye. Once the child and the classroom teacher are calm and can discuss the situation productively, the teacher comes to bring the child back to the classroom. Together they then solve the problems that led to the misbehavior.

(To learn more about using help from colleagues this way, see Yang and Charney 2005. To learn more about meeting with the student to solve behavior problems, see Charney 2004.)

APOLOGIZE IF NECESSARY

If all else fails and our anger unleashes unkind words, we should apologize. When we've regained composure, we should go to the child and say "I blew it. I said some mean things. I'm sorry." Then, we can work with the child to resolve any problem that may still need attention. If we're sincere in our apology, children do forgive. And, our genuine apology models for them a responsible way to fix a mistake.

REMINDING LANGUAGE IN ACTION

Reminders can be used to prepare children for success when they're about to start an activity, or to help them maintain appropriate behaviors during an activity. Transitions, independent work, interactive learning activities, and whole-group meetings are all times when reminders can come in handy. The following are examples of reminding language in each of these situations.

BEFORE TRANSITIONS

"What will you do to be ready for math quickly?"

"How can you make sure you have all the supplies you'll need?"

"Think about how you will help each other with cleanup."

"I'll be looking to see how you take care of our classroom supplies during cleanup."

"It's time for recess. What should you do before you go out?"

"What can you do to make it feel safe and friendly as we line up for lunch?"

"It's time for music. What should you do to get ready?"

DURING TRANSITIONS

"Ethan, what should you be doing right now?"

"Class, remind us how we're going to keep everyone safe."

"How did we decide we were going to line up?"

"Sara, show me how you can get ready quickly."

"I'll begin when everyone is ready."

BEFORE INDEPENDENT WORK

"Think about what you can do that will help you concentrate."

"What could you do if you have a question?"

"What if you get stuck?"

"How can you prepare so you won't have to get out of your seat until the work time is over?"

"What might be hard for you? What can you do that would help?"

DURING INDEPENDENT WORK

"Sean, what are you supposed to be doing right now?"

"What can you do that will help?"

"Remind us. How did we plan to take care of the books?"

"Show me how you will fix that."

"What's the next step in this work?"

BEFORE ACTIVITIES

"What might be hard about this activity? What might help you with the hard parts?"

"Who can show us a safe way to hold the [thermometers, rulers, markers, puzzles, etc.]?"

"How will you make sure everybody feels included?"

"How will you talk to each other about your work so that no one feels bad?"

"In this activity everyone will find a partner. What are some things you can do to help everybody feel included?"

"What will make it easy for girls and boys to work together as we do this activity?"

DURING ACTIVITIES

"I'm watching for all the ways you follow our classroom rules as you do this activity."

"Show me a safe way to do that."

"Safety rules, Graham!"

"Remind us. What's a friendly way to do that?"

"What will you do instead?"

"What kind of voices should we use?"

"What can you do if you don't understand something?"

BEFORE WHOLE-GROUP MEETINGS

"What are our meeting rules?"

"What can you do if you have an idea to share, but someone else is speaking?"

"How will you let the person who is speaking know that you are listening?"

"How do we disagree without put-downs?"

"What will help us have a good meeting?"

"Think about how you will help yourself do your best thinking and
learning."

DURING WHOLE-GROUP MEETINGS

"Meeting rules."

"I'm waiting for everyone to show they are ready to listen."

"Show what you'll do when you want a turn to talk."

"How can you say that in a friendly way?"

"What can you do with your hands and feet so Isaac can concentrate, Ursa?"

SUMMARY

Like reminders in everyday life, reminders in the classroom help students stay organized, on task, responsible, and safe. Reminders are most
effective when they're given before students embark on an undertaking
that may challenge their self-control or just as their behavior is veering
off course. In both situations, the teacher, rather than telling students
what they're supposed to do, prompts them to remember for themselves. This shows the teacher's faith in the students' desire and ability
to do the right thing and supports the children in developing a sense
of autonomy and competence.

WORKS CITED

Brady, Kathryn, Mary Beth Forton, Deborah Porter, and Chip Wood. 2003. *Rules in School.* Turners Falls, MA: Northeast Foundation for Children, Inc.

Charney, Ruth Sidney. 2002. *Teaching Children to Care.* Turners Falls, MA: Northeast Foundation for Children, Inc.

Charney, Ruth Sidney. 2004. "Teacher–Child Problem-Solving Conferences: Involving children in finding solutions to their behavior problems." *Responsive Classroom Newsletter.* Fall. *www.responsiveclassroom.org.*

Yang, Alice and Ruth Sidney Charney. 2005. "Buddy Teachers: Lending a hand to keep time-out positive and productive." *Responsive Classroom Newsletter.* Winter. *www.responsiveclassroom.org.*

CHAPTER SEVEN

Redirecting Language: Giving Clear Commands When Children Have Gone Off Track

A third grade class is doing an art project. Macy waves her scissors in the air, the point coming perilously close to a tablemate's face as she angrily explains why she won't share the scissors. "Macy, put the scissors down, now," her teacher tells her firmly.

Meanwhile, down the hall, Robin bursts through the entrance doors and races toward his classroom. "Robin, stop." Mr. Rice commands. When Robin stops and looks at him, Mr. Rice tells Robin, "Walk to your class."

On another day, a class of fifth graders is about to do some science experiments with balloons. Ms. Addison gathers them in a circle to review the scientific methods they're to use, then sends them off to their tables laid out with colorful balloons, powders, and other exciting materials. Immediately, some students start playing games with the balloons, games that quickly deteriorate into suggestive antics. Several students are completely ignoring the assignment, instead talking about who they like and don't like in the class. Ms. Addison looks around, rings the chime, and says firmly, "Stop. Everyone come back to the circle." Back in the circle, she clearly re-establishes the expectations for what the students are to do at the tables before sending them back for a second try.

Ideally, teachers spend most of their time reinforcing positive behaviors and giving reminders that allow students to recall how to behave. There are times, however, when we simply need to give students clear, non-negotiable commands about what to do, as in the above examples. When students are doing something dangerous to themselves or others, when they're too emotional to remember expectations and think reasonably about what they're supposed to be doing, or when they're otherwise too deeply invested in their off-track behavior to correct themselves, teachers should redirect them with firm words that tell them clearly and respectfully exactly what to do right now. Redirections literally change children's direction, mentally and usually physically as well. They tell children to sit down, move, change their tone, or make some other clear, visible change.

The skillful use of redirecting language allows us to provide the wise external control that keeps children on track when their self-control is failing them. It provides reassurance and a sense of safety, letting children know that the grownups are taking care of them. As my colleague Chip Wood used to reassure his students, "When you are not in control, I will be in control."

EFFECTIVE REDIRECTING LANGUAGE

Teachers give instructions many times every day. So what's there to learn about such a common type of communication? "You just tell the children what to do, don't you?" a friend asked when I told her I was writing about ways to redirect children. Yes, you do "just tell them what to do." But as most teachers know, a lot can go wrong when we tell children what to do when their emotions are heightened or when they're invested in the behavior that we want them to change. It takes knowledge and practice to redirect children in ways that get them to act differently while preserving their dignity and sense of belonging in the group. Here are some points to remember when using redirecting language:

* Be direct and specific.

* Name the desired behavior.

* Keep it brief.

* Phrase redirections as a statement, not a question.

* Follow through after giving a redirection.

BE DIRECT AND SPECIFIC: "DAVID, HANDS IN YOUR LAP."

A second grade teacher observes her class as they begin to share their work on an assignment. She notices David looking excited and waving his hands around wildly, almost hitting neighboring children accidentally as he hums to himself. The teacher walks over to David and quietly but firmly says, "David, hands in your lap."

There are two things to notice about this teacher's wording. First, she addresses David directly. If David's hands are waving about wildly, he is not likely to be in a state of mind to understand indirect communications such as "Someone needs to get his hands under control." Hearing this, David might wonder, "Who out of all the class is this someone?" If he does understand that his teacher is sending an indirect message to him, he may feel embarrassed because the whole class has been invited to observe his misbehavior while he himself was the last to know. Embarrassment may easily turn into rebellion, a corroding of a sense of belonging and competence in the class, and a souring of the student's relationship with his teacher.

By contrast, "David, hands in your lap" gets David's attention quickly and less publicly. He is swiftly redirected to more positive behavior before the misbehavior becomes a public disturbance and a matter of public attention. And the teacher has maintained a friendly and respectful relationship with David.

The second thing to notice about this teacher's language is that she tells David exactly what to do. "Hands in your lap" is much more specific than something such as "Get your hands under control." In his distracted state, David may not be sure how he is to get his "hands under control." He may even feel that his hands are under control because they're doing exactly what he wants them to do.

But don't we want to help children make the connection between "being in control" and the actual behavior of keeping their hands in their lap? Don't we want them to learn what ideas such as "respectful," "successful," and "inclusive" mean by thinking about how to apply them in the situation they're in? Yes, but not when their self-control is shaky or gone. Helping children connect abstract terms with concrete behaviors is productive when we give them reminders or reinforcements—both of which are done when the children are calm and aren't already in the midst of misbehavior. (See Chapters 5 and 6 to learn about reinforcing and reminding language.) When they're in the midst of misbehavior, emotionally riled up, or jeopardizing other students' sense of safety, belonging, or significance, we should waste no time and tell children exactly and clearly what to do.

This redirection needs to be delivered in a calm, even tone, not an angry one. A calm, even tone conveys that we respect the children even when we don't condone their behavior.

EXAMPLES OF USING DIRECT, SPECIFIC REDIRECTING LANGUAGE

Instead of:	Try:
"Sit in a place where you can be successful."	"Sit at another table where you can pay attention to your work."
"We don't have maid service here."	"Clean up your work area."

Instead of:	Try:
"I don't want to have to remind you about our math routine."	"Bring your math books."
"It sounds like somebody needs to work harder."	"Casey, it's time to do this assignment right now."
"Do you want me to take those toys away?"	"Put those toys away."
"Be nice."	"Help Evan clean up the paper."

NAME THE DESIRED BEHAVIOR: "ALL EYES ON MIRANDA."

Redirections work best when they name the wanted rather than the unwanted behavior. Miranda is sharing her work. As I look around at a group of children whispering with each other and looking out the windows, I feel impatient. We've discussed, modeled, and practiced respectful listening. My first impulse now is to describe the problem. "We're losing your attention here," I want to admonish. Or I'm tempted to ask a rhetorical question and to scold: "Why are you all whispering to each other? You know better!" But I resist the impulse, knowing that those words would only sound like a complaint or an attack on children's character, which would make students fearful or defensive. Besides, while the embedded indirect request to pay attention to Miranda might be clear to some students, more likely it'll be lost on most. I know the group's behavior is jeopardizing Miranda's sense of safety and belonging with her classmates. What's called for here is a fast and efficient redirection.

So, rather than describing the problem, I name what I want the children to do by saying "All eyes on Miranda." "All eyes on Miranda" does not require that the distracted students make any inferences about what they are to do. It wastes no time complaining about the behavior and avoids implying anything about students' character. Instead, it clearly commands students to show respectful behavior. Respect for classmates who are sharing is a clear and firm expectation in this classroom. When it is not adhered to, I get the students back on track as quickly and positively as possible by telling them exactly what to do.

Getting into the habit of naming the desired behavior can take time. I struggled with it when I first started trying to change my teacher language. Especially in frustrating or heated moments, my tendency was to name the unwanted behavior. The key to breaking this habit, I found, was to stop and think before I gave any redirection. If I didn't want Elena to complain, what did I want her to do instead? Just by asking myself that question, I could usually articulate the positive behavior I expected. I'd come up with, "Elena, tell me what would help" or "It's time to get to work." Sam's not following directions. What do I want him to do? I want him to read the directions on page three. So I say to him, "Go back and read the directions on page three again."

To be sure, this change didn't take place cleanly overnight. Even after I began naming only the wanted behavior, I would sometimes catch myself slipping back to something like "There's too much chatter in here. Stop talking so much." But if that happened, I would stop and think, then change direction (giving myself a mental redirection) and add, "It's time to write quietly now." That way at least I named for students both the unwanted and wanted behavior. Over time the positive directions came to mind much more spontaneously. I spent less and less time telling children what not to do, and more and more time directing them toward what to do.

EXAMPLES OF NAMING THE DESIRED BEHAVIOR

Instead of:	Try:
"Stop running!"	"Stop. Walk."
"Lots of you are wasting time."	"We'll begin when you're all seated with your folder on your desk."
"These tables are a mess."	"Clean off your tables before you line up."
"Why are you moving before you've gotten directions?"	"Stop. Wait to hear the directions."

Instead of:	Try:
"How many times do I have to say 'No talking right now'?"	"It's time to listen."
"Why aren't you lined up yet?"	"Everyone line up and face forward."

KEEP IT BRIEF: "BOOKS CLOSED. EYES AND EARS ON ME."

I remember an incident in one of my third grade classrooms—one of many such scenes from my early teaching days. The children were enthusiastically collecting books about insects from the classroom library, thumbing through the pages and then leaving the volumes discarded here and there on their way to finding more books. In their delight, the children had forgotten the expectations for caring for the books, which we had so carefully established and reviewed before they began the activity. The room was in chaos. "Alright, everyone, listen up. This is not working!" I said, or actually, yelled. I continued, "You've got to put away the books you already have out before you get another one. Otherwise they'll get lost or hurt and we won't have them to read anymore. That would be a shame, and it would be hard to do the insect projects without the books to get information from." A few children began to put some books away, but most continued with what they had been doing. My exasperation escalated. Why weren't the children listening to me? Didn't they understand? Didn't I give my reasoning fully?

Well, yes, I later realized. I did give my reasoning fully, and that was the problem. I wanted the students not only to behave in ways that helped them learn and care for the books, but also to understand why some behaviors were more productive than others and how not following established expectations affected them personally. The problem was that in the midst of their enthusiastic chaos, the children were not prepared to listen to and follow all this reasoning. It would've been more effective to get their attention with a few direct words: "Books closed. Eyes and ears on me." Once the books were closed and the children were paying attention to me, then I could give the next direction. And that one should also be brief and specific: "Put all the books away carefully." Only after they'd done this would the children be ready to think with me about why leaving books all over the room was a problem.

When children need redirection, the fewer words we use, the better. Giving only one, or at most two, directions at a time is important. This keeps our language action oriented and easy to take in.

Sometimes when children are well into off-track behavior, simply commanding "Freeze!" or "Stop!" is a good place to start. Once the children are quiet and still, they are ready for our next instruction. Another way to get children's attention quickly is to use an established nonverbal signal such as the teacher's raised hand, a bell or chime, or flipping a light switch off and on.

Whatever the word or signal, it's best to start early in the year to teach it as a regular classroom routine. Explain that the word or signal means "Stop, look at me, listen." Then practice with the class so students will be familiar with it the next time you need to get their attention.

Many teachers try to get the class's attention by saying "Shhh!" While this can be a simple and effective way to signal a small, informal group, my experience is that it doesn't work all that well with a class. The sound doesn't carry past the few closest people, so to achieve complete quiet the teacher would have to walk around the whole room shhh-ing. Often the teacher's shhh-ing gets everyone shhh-ing instead of getting everyone quiet. This signal also relies on the teacher using her or his voice to overpower the children's, which sends the unintended message that the teacher gains control or authority by overpowering the children. A nonverbal signal that's been well established and practiced gets around all these problems.

PHRASE REDIRECTIONS AS A STATEMENT, NOT A QUESTION: "LINE UP NOW" RATHER THAN "COULD YOU ALL LINE UP NOW?"

Mr. Deckert, a fifth grade teacher, had a habit of phrasing redirections as questions. Like many teachers, including myself earlier in my teaching career, he would say to students, "Could you all line up quickly now?" or "Could you get out your books?" Sometimes he phrased the redirections as announcements of what he'd like to request or as a suggestion, as in "I'm going to ask you to sit over here" or "I suggest you save that conversation for later and focus on your writing right now."

When I pointed this out to him, he was surprised. He wasn't aware that he was using questions or suggestions to give redirections. It was an unconscious habit. After thinking about it for awhile, Mr. Deckert defended this practice. "I'm modeling politeness," he told me. "After all, I wouldn't say to you, 'Pass the salt.' I would say, 'Would you please pass the salt?' Instead of 'Sit down,' I would say, 'Will you have a seat?'"

It's true that in our society we commonly soften directions to adults by phrasing them as questions or suggestions. It's understood that this is a way to respect others' sense of dignity. And it's understood that when we are asked to sit, we are generally expected to sit. Mr. Deckert's intention was good, stemming from respect for the children and a desire to teach them positive social skills. This is no doubt the intention of all teachers who soften redirections into questions.

However, the purpose of teachers' professional use of redirections is different from the purpose of conversations among adults. The purpose of redirection is to guide a child who is not currently able to guide his or her own behaviors wisely. In such moments, children need firm limits, not words that give the illusion of choice when we're not really offering any choice. It's more respectful and effective at such times to say exactly what we mean. In these situations, calm, direct statements to children are not impolite.

"But won't children, like adults, understand the context of our questions or suggestions, and therefore know they're really directions?" some teachers ask. Some children will, but enough won't. Enough will take our words literally to make this kind of language a problem. For the literal understanders, the questions may cause confusion. A teacher says, "Will you have a seat?" "Well, I don't really want to have a seat. Seems like not having a seat is an option," the child might think. The student continues to mill about the room, and then is as surprised by the teacher's anger as the teacher is by the child's refusal to sit down.

Then there are some students who know that a question is intended to be a direction, but will take the teacher's indirect language as an opening to say "No" and engage in a power struggle.

Another way teachers soften redirections is to use "please" and "thank you." "Please turn around and listen" or "Thank you for working on your assignment," we may say.

There are certainly times when it's appropriate to use "please" and "thank you" with students, but not when we're redirecting behavior. We generally use "please" when asking someone to do us a favor and "thank you" to indicate gratitude for a favor done. When we give re-directions, we're not asking students to support us or do us a favor. Rather, we're guiding them toward positive behavior for their own learning and growth. Using "please" and "thank you" would therefore send the confusing message that students are to behave to please us.

Similarly, the phrase "for me"—as in "Line up over here for me" and "Finish your work for me"—can send the wrong message to students. By implying that the goal is to please the teacher, such language undermines students' efforts to develop self-control and their sense of autonomy.

It's important to remember that calm, direct statements to children do not model rudeness. When we truly respect the children, they will be able to hear that respect in our directions and retain their sense of dignity.

EXAMPLES OF REPLACING QUESTIONS AND SUGGESTIONS WITH STATEMENTS

Instead of:	Try:
"Would you come sit by me?"	"Come sit by me."
"I'm going to ask table one to quiet down."	"Table one, quiet down."
"Will you look at me?"	"Eyes on me."
"Can you put your backpacks away?"	"All backpacks on their hooks."
"Will you please concentrate?"	"It's time to read your book now."

Instead of:	Try:
"Will you get ready to work for me?"	"I will begin when everyone has supplies out and is ready to listen for directions."
"I suggest you put those back where they belong."	"Put the game cards away now."

FOLLOW THROUGH AFTER GIVING A REDIRECTION

If redirections are to be the firm limits they are meant to be, we have to see to it that children act on them. This means taking time to observe the children and stepping in with clearer directions or a logical consequence if children don't follow our redirection.

When David's teacher told him to put his hands in his lap, she watched to see that he did so. If he didn't, she would have taken another step: If it seemed that being near his classmates was stimulating the hand waving, she might have told David to move to a seat away from them and closer to her, and then waited until he was resettled with hands in his lap before engaging with the class. If it seemed that David needed some time and space to calm down, she might have told him to take a short time-out in a place away from the action. If the teacher believed that David was too absorbed in his hand waving to comprehend her direction, she might have simply directed him again, but even more concisely: "David, stop," she might have said, then repeated her original instruction when she was sure of his attention.

By following through after giving redirections, we tell students that we mean what we say and that when we set limits, they are firm. Students learn that when they hear a redirection, they are to act.

A common practice among teachers is to give students a redirection and tell them, in the same breath, what the consequence will be if they don't heed it. "Finish your work or you'll lose recess time," we say, or "Stop or you'll lose your computer time." Perhaps what's behind this way of speaking is our worry that without telling students the consequence, our redirection will have no teeth. Our intention may

Using "Sir," "Miss," and "Ma'am": Examine Your Intentions

Teachers sometimes ask whether they should address children as "sir," miss," or "ma'am" when redirecting children, or speaking with them in any context, for that matter. In my opinion, it depends. The terms "sir," "miss," and "ma'am" indicate respect for someone who is in authority. As a child growing up in the American South, I learned to say "ma'am" and "sir" to all adults or risk punishment. Teachers may say to students, "Walk in the hall, sir," "Take a break, ma'am," or "Miss Amy, it's time to concentrate on your writing" as a way to model showing respect or to make the point that students have some authority at school.

But while it's true that children should have authority over some aspects of their activities and possessions in the classroom, teachers must maintain authority when it comes to establishing and maintaining firm limits for children's behavior. I therefore think that the use of "sir," "miss," or "ma'am" when directing or redirecting children can come across as ironic or possibly even sarcastic.

The important thing, I believe, is for teachers to think honestly about why they're using these terms. That will help them judge whether their use is appropriate and respectful of children.

be to make sure students know what they'll be getting into if they don't get back to the expected behaviors. But the teaching of logical consequences is best done at calm times starting from the very beginning of the school year. As long as that teaching happens and students are familiar with the limits and the consequences, we don't need to warn them of the "or else" when we redirect them. The "teeth" come from our action: the fact that we indeed follow through with logical consequences if students don't change course after our redirection.

In fact, not only is saying the "or else" unnecessary, it can actually do harm because rather than communicating faith in the children's desire and ability to do the right thing, it communicates the opposite: an expectation that students will not or cannot do the right thing unless threatened with something loathsome. Warnings can also provoke power struggles because they emphasize the teacher's power over the children.

REDIRECTING LANGUAGE IN ACTION

Redirection is always used as a response to off-track behavior. Ideally, it is used sparingly as a way to support children when their self-control is not in place. If you find yourself using a lot of redirections during an activity or transition, it may be time to stop the action, give the children a chance to calm down, and then review and practice expectations once again. Then, do plenty of reinforcing and reminding as they practice.

Here are some examples of redirections that teachers might use during group sessions, independent work sessions, and transitions.

GROUP SESSIONS

"Hands down until the speaker has finished talking."

"Stop and think. Then raise your hands if you have an idea."

"It's time to listen now."

"Use quiet voices."

"Tell your feet to hold still."

"Look at the chart."

INDEPENDENT WORK SESSIONS

"Scissors are for cutting paper only."

"Take turns with the markers."

"It's time to sit at your table and work now."

"Pick up the paper on the floor."

"Find a place to work where you can concentrate and finish the job."

"Use kind words."

"The rulers are for sharing."

TRANSITIONS

"Stop. Finish cleanup now."

"When you've pushed your chairs in and lined up, we can go."

"Freeze." Then, "Get your shoes for gym."

"Carry the scissors safely."

"When you have put your books away, we'll begin."

"Walk."

"Help John clean up."

SUMMARY

Sometimes teachers need to give students clear, non-negotiable commands. It may be because the students are doing something dangerous, because they're too emotional at the moment to exercise self-control, or because they're too far along in off-track behavior to pull themselves back without teacher guidance. At these times, the teacher uses redirecting language: a short statement or phrase that tells students respectfully, directly, and specifically what to do. There is no discussion and no lecturing or explanations from the teacher. Skillfully used, redirecting language brings students back to safe and positive behavior while respecting their sense of dignity.

Putting It All Together

It's a typical early fall day in Ms. Dempske's third grade class. The children have just finished an independent writing period and are scurrying to store writing folders, return pencils to containers, and put snacks away to get ready for reading time. As the children finish putting their materials away, Ms. Dempske waits for them in her chair at the meeting rug. One by one and two by two the children come to the rug, finding a place to sit in a circle. When most of the children are seated, Ms. Dempske says, "When everyone is ready to listen, I'll begin."

After a minute the last stragglers find a place in the circle, sit, and look at their teacher. "I see empty hands and calm bodies. I see your eyes on me. We are ready for reading time," Ms. Dempske says in a kind and steady voice.

"This year I hope that you will all love reading and come to see yourselves as good readers. You know, you don't have to be able to read big, hard words or long chapter books to be a good reader and enjoy books. All you need is to think like good readers," Ms. Dempske tells the children.

"Yesterday, when I read *Lester's Dog* to you, I noticed that many of you were thinking like good readers. Some of you made predictions about what you thought would happen next. I remember Hamilton predicted that the dog would chase the kitten. And what happened, Hamilton?" Ms. Dempske grins.

"I was right! I knew it!"

"Yes, and you were also doing some careful noticing. You noticed when the boys found the kitten, and you knew that dogs often chase cats. So you were noticing things about the story and making connections."

Ms. Dempske continues, "Some of you were making connections with the story the way Lynnetta did when she shared how her dog was like Lester's dog. You were noticing details about the story and you were wondering. I remember that Chavon wondered what a hearing aid was. That's the kind of thinking that good readers do."

Noticing that Amy has picked up the book *Lester's Dog* from its display stand, Ms. Dempske pauses a moment and looks directly at Amy. Amy continues to flip pages in the book. "The book goes in the stand, Amy," the teacher directs. Amy looks up at her, then places the book back in its holder.

Ms. Dempske resumes, "Today I expect all of you to be good readers again, readers who enjoy and learn from reading. You'll all begin reading the book that you selected as your 'just right book,' a book that you are interested in, and that you can read most of the words in, so it makes sense to you. Before we begin reading, what are some things you can do that will help you think like a good reader?"

"You have to be able to concentrate on the book," offers Meredith.

"Maybe put things away on the tables so only the book is out and we don't play around with things," adds Chavon.

"If you go to read on the rug, don't sit next to someone you'll want to talk to," says Connie, glancing at her best friend, Sahreem.

"What else do people who want to read on the rug need to think about?" asks Ms. Dempske.

"Only six kids at a time," says Carla.

"If you're sitting on the rug, better sit where it's comfortable!" adds Henry. "Yesterday I sat against the bookshelves, and it hurt my back!"

"So you need to think carefully about putting away distractions and where you sit," Ms. Dempske summarizes.

"Look at the pictures," Jake adds. "That helps you think about it."

"Okay, sounds like you're ready to be good readers. Here's a question for you to think about as you read." Ms. Dempske turns to write the question on the board as she speaks the words: "What things in my life does this reading remind me of?"

"I'll be watching as you get started." Ms. Dempske says.

In just a few short moments, this teacher skillfully used language to engage, inspire, and support children's learning. She used envisioning, open-ended questioning, reinforcing, reminding, and redirecting language. She listened and paraphrased. She kept her words succinct and her tone warm and firm. She used silence when appropriate. Her words and tone communicated her belief that the students were capable, motivated, and well-intentioned. Her language helped create a positive learning experience for the children. This is how school can sound.

APPENDIX A

Examples of Effective Teacher Language

Examples from this book, gathered here for quick reference

APPENDIX B

The Process of Developing More Effective Teacher Language

Typical stages in language change, with strategies for success

Examples of Effective Teacher Language

ENVISIONING LANGUAGE

SETTING A POSITIVE TONE FOR FUTURE WORK

"Good morning, scientists! I'm looking forward this year to helping you discover answers to some of the mysteries about the way our world works."

"This year I hope our classroom will be a safe and caring place to learn and that everyone will be able to do their best work."

"We've been sharing with each other about animals we like, sports we play, and our other interests. I expect all of you will choose something you're interested in and do such great research on it that you become the class expert on your topic. You'll be able to answer questions about your topic or have a good idea how to find the answer."

ENGAGING CHILDREN IN PROBLEM SOLVING

"So what can you do to figure out who will be flag guard in such a way that Capture the Flag can be fun for everybody and you can run fast, try to outsmart the other team, and help teammates?"

"You're tired of the word 'respectful.' Seems like the teachers use it a lot just to make you listen to them. What if 'respectful' really did mean something important to you? What would be happening for you at school if you genuinely felt respected by each other?"

"We can do our best learning when we are careful listeners. What do careful listeners do?"

NAMING POSITIVE IDENTITIES FOR CHILDREN

"I'm so excited to be your reading teacher this year. My hope is that by the end of this year you will all be book lovers! I hope each of you discovers at least one book that you love so much, sometimes you'd rather read it than watch TV!"

"Good writers write about what they're interested in and know well. I'm looking forward to learning more about what is important to you as you write today."

"I see that our classroom is full of good thinkers who are ready to learn! This year, I expect that all of you will find some school-work that you'll be able to do easily and some that will require hard work. But we're all good thinkers, so we're all going to learn a lot!"

USING CONCRETE IMAGES AND WORDS THAT CHILDREN USE

"Everyone here has a right to feel okay about themselves. When you're in this class, each of you should be able to feel okay about what you wear, the work you do, and what you look like. What needs to happen so everyone can feel okay when they're here?"

"The most important reason we're doing this is to have fun. When we sing and clap in a happy way, and when we let each other sing and clap in their happy way, we'll all have fun—and look like stars to boot!"

USING METAPHORS

"Let's pretend we're looking through magic spyglasses at our class-room. We're looking at our classroom when it's a safe and welcoming place for everybody and we're all doing our best learning. What kinds of things do you see? What are you doing?"

"You are ready to take another step up the mountain. We're going on a field trip tomorrow. You're going to show you can take care of yourselves and each other in unfamiliar surroundings. What are some ways you'll do that?"

LETTING CHILDREN FILL IN THE DETAILS

"What does being a class expert look and sound like? What would I be doing if I were an expert on my topic?"

"Imagine a book that you could love so much that you'd rather read it than watch TV. What might you find in such a book?"

"What would a math group that you'd enjoy be like? What would you see and hear? How would you feel?"

OPEN-ENDED QUESTIONS

QUESTIONS FOR DIFFERENT PURPOSES

		CLASSROOM SITUATION		
		Introducing a lesson or activity	**During and at the close of a lesson or activity**	**Solving behavioral problems**
PURPOSE	**Increasing awareness of knowledge**	"What do you know about [birds, fairy tales, folk songs, basketball, rivers, etc.]?" "Where have you heard or read about this topic before?"	"What have you learned so far?" "How does this [map, letter, phrase, etc.] compare to that one?" "How could you put that into your own words?"	"What happened?" "What did you notice?" "How might an observer describe what happened?" "What would be an example?"
PURPOSE	**Generating interest**	"What do you notice about [this poem, this ball, this book, etc.]?" "What do you wonder about when it comes to this topic?"	"What part of this do you find most interesting?" "What else might you want to try?" "What more would you like to know about this?"	"What questions do you have?" "What surprised you?" "What do you notice that's new to you?"

CLASSROOM SITUATION		
Introducing a lesson or activity	**During and at the close of a lesson or activity**	**Solving behavioral problems**

PURPOSE

Making personal connections

"How do you feel when you [hear a fairy tale, try a new sport, etc.]?" "When have you used [a microscope, rules, comparisons, etc.] before?" "When might you use [a song, this game, journal writing, etc.] to help you learn something?"	"What about this is especially interesting to you?" "How might this information help you [when you need to find a book, the next time you take the subway, when we visit the nature center]?" "What part would you especially want to remember?"	"What does this remind you of?" "How have you seen people use this skill?"

Hearing classmates' ideas

"How might we use [the computer, the microscope, etc.] to help us learn about [minerals, adjectives, great paintings, etc.]?" "What could you do if you forget the directions?"	"What are some ways you all figured that out?" "What are some questions you might ask when you do your interviews? Let's see how many ideas we can come up with as a class." "What are some possible ideas?"	"What are some possible reasons why people [call names, tease, don't finish work, etc.]?" "How does this compare to your experience? Let's hear from all of you."

Identifying or clarifying problems

"What problems could possibly come up when you do this?" "What might be hard for some people?"	"How's it going?" "Where are you stuck?" "How would you describe the problem?" "How could you possibly find out?"	"What's an example of this kind of problem?" "Where else do you see this problem happening?" "What might be going on in some kids' minds when they think about this?"

CLASSROOM SITUATION		
Introducing a lesson or activity	**During and at the close of a lesson or activity**	**Solving behavioral problems**
"What could you do if [you think you're running out of time, you're stuck for ideas, etc.]?" "When would be good times to ask for help?"	"Which [book, color, eraser, block, etc.] do you think might work better for you?" "What might help?" "Where could you look for ideas?"	"How might someone solve that problem?" "Who could help?" "What else might work?"
"How will you make sure to [finish on time, do every step, take care of each other, etc.]?" "What materials do you need to gather before you start?"	"What's your plan?" "What might someone's next move be?" "What's one thing you might do first?"	"What might a kid in that situation do differently next time?" "What might you do next?" "Which step feels like the right one to try first?"
"How long do you think you will need?" "How will you decide whom to work with?"	"Why might some students choose this [strategy, object, tool, etc.] over the others?" "What's working for you?" "What's hard for you?"	"What might be a good way to know if your plan is working?" "How could someone know if this is their best work?" "What helped you concentrate well today?"

Row labels (PURPOSE): Generating possible solutions / Planning next steps / Evaluating a plan or process

ARTICULATING BOUNDARIES IN
OPEN-ENDED QUESTIONS

Instead of:	Try:
"How could you use the globe?"	"How could you use the globe to discover facts about continents?"
"What kinds of things might you do on the field trip?"	"What kinds of things might you do on the field trip that will help you learn and keep you safe?"
"What are some ways you could solve that problem?"	"What are some ways you could solve that problem using the supplies in our classroom?"

DE-EMPHASIZING COMPETITION
WHEN ASKING QUESTIONS

Instead of:	Try:
"Who knows a good way to use the clay?"	"What are some different ways we might use the clay?"
"How can we make this graph the most beautiful?"	"What are some different ways to make this graph beautiful?"
"Whose drawing do you think is best? Why?"	"What good ideas do you see in the different ways people did their drawings?"
"Kerry, what strategies for writing neatly can you suggest to the others?"	"What strategies might help someone write more neatly?"
"Who has a better idea?"	"Who has a different idea?"

REFERRING TO CONCRETE EXPERIENCES

Instead of:	Try:
"How would you describe your writing?"	"What are some things you like about the character sketch you did of your sister?"
"What are some ways you could be a better student?"	"What did you do during today's partner share that helped you learn?"
"How do you feel about your math work?"	"What about this morning's math assignment makes you proud?"
"What do good scientists do?"	"What are some ways to be good scientists when we observe our worm farm today?"
"How do responsible people act?"	"What does it look like when people are responsible in the cafeteria?"

LISTENING—PAUSING AND PARAPHRASING

DURING INDEPENDENT WORK TIME

Teacher: Danae, you've been really focused on your book. What's so interesting?

Danae (grinning): I just think it's really funny and interesting that a mouse can ride around on a motorcycle.

Pause

Teacher: So, you're intrigued with the fantasy part of it?

Danae: Yeah, I guess so. And also it's interesting to think about how a mouse would see the things that people think are just normal.

Pause

Teacher: Kind of gives you a different perspective, huh?

Danae: Yeah.

DURING INDIVIDUAL PROBLEM SOLVING

Teacher: Robert, I've noticed that you've been arguing a lot with some of the kids. What have you noticed?

Pause

Robert: Well, a little bit with Rudy and Maurice, I guess.

Pause

Teacher: Tell me more about that.

Robert: Rudy and Maurice are just always picking on me. They don't like me, so I don't like them.

Pause

Teacher: So it seems like Rudy and Maurice are being mean for no reason.

Robert: Yeah.

Pause

Robert: And sometimes I'm mean to them, too.

Pause

Teacher: Oh. So, you think sometimes they might have a reason?

Robert: Well, sometimes.

Pause

Teacher: Tell me more about when you are mean to them. What do you do?

DURING A GROUP DISCUSSION

Teacher: What are some things you know about deserts?

Pause

Manny: They're very dry and brown.

Pause

Samika: Lots of sand, I think.

Brianna: Some deserts have cactuses and they are green. Sometimes they have flowers.

Pause

Jerry: Deserts are deserts because they get hardly any rain. And they're hot.

Manny: Deserts can be cold at night. I was in a desert when it was cold.

Surea: Deserts can have flowers in them.

Pause

Leah: Deserts can have camels. And people who live in tents.

Pause

Teacher: So deserts are dry and sandy, but they also have plants and animals and even people in them. What else do you know or think you might know about deserts?

DURING GROUP PROBLEM SOLVING

Teacher: I've been noticing that lots of you are having difficulty getting your homework done on time. What might be some reasons that people have a hard time getting their homework done?

Pause

Alejandra: Sometimes the homework is too hard and they don't know how to do it.

Pause

David: If you can't do it and you don't have anyone to help you, it's hard.

Rickie: I have to go to my Grandma's after school and there's lots of little kids yelling and Grandma wants me to play with them 'cause she's tired. And then I'm too tired for homework!

Tory: My cousins are always rowdy and it's hard to concentrate.

Pause

Michael: I have Little League right after school and by the time we get home it's late.

Pause

Teacher: It sounds like some kids find it hard to concentrate after school, some don't have the help they need, and some have other things to do. What kinds of things might help kids get homework done when they're finding it hard to concentrate?

REINFORCING LANGUAGE

REPLACING GENERAL PRAISE WITH SPECIFIC DESCRIPTION

Instead of:	Try:
"Good job!"	"I notice you used a simile here that helps the reader feel how tense the scene was."
"This is A+ work!"	"You paid attention to every detail in this model."
"Beautiful!"	"You made all the spaces in the grid even and used two contrasting colors. That makes this graph easy for readers to take in."
"Nice!"	"I see that all the backpacks and coats have been put away neatly."

NAMING CONCRETE, SPECIFIC BEHAVIORS

Instead of:	Try:
"Your spelling shows progress."	"You remembered to change the 'y' to 'i' when adding 'ed.'"
"Terrific meeting today!"	"I noticed lots of careful listening and pausing to think before talking."
"Nice job with your note taking."	"I see you wrote the main ideas in your own words and carefully noted where you got the information."
"I noticed how hard you worked."	"You kept working on this a long time. And when you didn't know the answer right away, you tried a different strategy or asked someone for help."

EMPHASIZING DESCRIPTION OVER
PERSONAL APPROVAL

Instead of:	Try:
"I'm so pleased with the way you all helped each other with cleanup so you could finish faster."	"You all helped each other with cleanup so you could finish faster."
"Thank you for your thoughtful suggestions to the younger students."	"You gave thoughtful suggestions to the younger students. I'm sure they found them helpful."
"I love how quiet the room was and how busily everyone was working."	"Did you notice how quiet the room was and how busily everyone was working?"
"I like how you made these all different sizes."	"You made these all different sizes. Why did you do that?"

ENCOURAGING WITHOUT ELEVATING
INDIVIDUALS

Instead of:	Try:
"I like the way Reid and Tran followed the directions. Who else?"	"I see some names on the sign-up board. Who can remind us of the sign-up procedure."
"Notice how Liselle put her backpack and coat in the cubby so they both fit? Let's see if everyone can do that."	"I notice that all the backpacks and coats are in the general cubby area. What else could we do to make that area even neater?"
"Let's see which table can get their supplies together the fastest."	"I see lots of supplies being gathered. We'll begin when every table is ready."
"Yesterday, Group 1 took twelve seconds to move their chairs into the circle. Let's see if you all can do it just as quickly."	"Yesterday, you all cut two seconds off your chair-moving time. Let's see if we can set a class record today."

MORE EXAMPLES OF REINFORCING LANGUAGE

DURING TRANSITIONS

"I see trash going into trash cans. I see backpacks put away."

"Lots of you are playing the quiet hand game we learned to help us through waiting time."

"You got to the rug for dismissal in forty-seven seconds. That's a record!"

"Yesterday it took eight minutes for everyone to settle down with a book after recess. Today it only took five. What caused the difference?"

"I noticed that when I gave the three minute warning, lots of you started wrapping up and putting your folders in the bin."

DURING GROUP ACTIVITIES

"Did you notice how many facts we listed about vernal pools? This class knows a lot about that topic!"

"Listen to the respectful words you're using!"

"I noticed people giving supportive clues. What are some other things you noticed that made this activity go well?"

"You brought clipboards and pencils. That's one way to remember the ideas from this discussion."

"A few weeks ago we had only one street and four buildings in our model town. Now we have many streets and nearly twenty-five buildings."

DURING INDEPENDENT WORK TIME

"You used several sound words in this poem. It helps the reader 'hear' what you're describing."

"Lots of good interview questions being jotted down."

"I see you're checking your work before turning it in."

"You decided to use different colors this time. What was your thinking there?"

"Many of you are remembering to put the books back in their original bins so others can find them."

"Oh, I see you're using chapter headings in your writing. You seem to be picking up something from the books you're reading."

"So many problems done! You're getting fast with multiplication."

IN ONE-ON-ONE CONVERSATIONS

"You showed kindness during recess yesterday when you asked Didi to join the game."

"I notice you're speaking more loudly in discussions. That helps us know your ideas."

"Remember when you thought fractions were really hard? Today you did all the fractions problems with no trouble."

"You and Tamika exchanged some good ideas today. What made that go so well?"

"You've been taking risks in the skits by accepting harder roles. How does that feel?"

"I notice you stayed quieter today so your tablemates could talk more."

REMINDING LANGUAGE

USING NEUTRAL WORDING AND TONE

Instead of:	Try:
"What would you be doing now if you had listened to directions?"	"What do the directions say to do now, Jeremy?"
"Why don't you figure out how you'll clean up?"	"How will you clean up?"
"Why aren't you including both partners' ideas?"	"What are some things you can do so both partners' ideas are included?"

KEEP REMINDERS BRIEF

Instead of:	Try:
"We're going to join other classes in a few minutes for all-school meeting. We've talked about how we can be in control of ourselves when we're with other classes, and we've practiced. I want to see all of you remember what we learned. Who remembers how we show self-control?"	"We'll be going to all-school meeting in a few minutes. How will we show self-control?"
"Mia, you look like you're stuck on this problem. When you're stuck, are you supposed to make noises that distract others? Do you remember what we said about what to do when you're stuck?"	"Mia, what can you do if you get stuck on a problem?"
"Austin, you're going to hurt someone flinging the stick like that! Didn't we go over this? Were you listening?"	"Austin, safety rules."
"Before we start this meeting, I want everyone to think about being considerate and respectful in meetings because last week our meetings could've gone better. We have to do better this week."	"Before we start the meeting, let's review. What will help us have a good meeting?"

MORE EXAMPLES OF REMINDING LANGUAGE

BEFORE TRANSITIONS

"What will you do to be ready for math quickly?"

"How can you make sure you have all the supplies you'll need?"

"Think about how you will help each other with cleanup."

"I'll be looking to see how you take care of our classroom supplies during cleanup."

"It's time for recess. What should you do before you go out?"

"What can you do to make it feel safe and friendly as we line up for lunch?"

"It's time for music. What should you do to get ready?"

DURING TRANSITIONS

"Ethan, what should you be doing right now?"

"Class, remind us how we're going to keep everyone safe."

"How did we decide we were going to line up?"

"Sara, show me how you can get ready quickly."

"I'll begin when everyone is ready."

BEFORE INDEPENDENT WORK

"Think about what you can do that will help you concentrate."

"What could you do if you have a question?"

"What if you get stuck?"

"How can you prepare so you won't have to get out of your seat until the work time is over?"

"What might be hard for you? What can you do that would help?"

DURING INDEPENDENT WORK

"Sean, what are you supposed to be doing right now?"

"What can you do that will help?"

"Remind us. How did we plan to take care of the books?"

"Show me how you will fix that."

"What's the next step in this work?"

BEFORE ACTIVITIES

"What might be hard about this activity? What might help you with the hard parts?"

"Who can show us a safe way to hold the [thermometers, rulers, markers, puzzles, etc.]?"

"How will you make sure everybody feels included?"

"How will you talk to each other about your work so that no one feels bad?"

"In this activity everyone will find a partner. What are some things you can do to help everybody feel included?"

"What will make it easy for girls and boys to work together as we do this activity?"

DURING ACTIVITIES

"I'm watching for all the ways you follow our classroom rules as you do this activity."

"Show me a safe way to do that."

"Safety rules, Graham!"

"Remind us. What's a friendly way to do that?"

"What will you do instead?"

"What kind of voices should we use?"

"What can you do if you don't understand something?"

BEFORE WHOLE-GROUP MEETINGS

"What are our meeting rules?"

"What can you do if you have an idea to share, but someone else is speaking?"

"How will you let the person who is speaking know that you are listening?"

"How do we disagree without put-downs?"

"What will help us have a good meeting?"

"Think about how you will help yourself do your best thinking and
learning."

DURING WHOLE-GROUP MEETINGS

"Meeting rules."

"I'm waiting for everyone to show they are ready to listen."

"Show what you'll do when you want a turn to talk."

"How can you say that in a friendly way?"

"What can you do with your hands and feet so Isaac can concentrate, Ursa?"

REDIRECTING LANGUAGE

USING DIRECT, SPECIFIC REDIRECTING LANGUAGE

Instead of:	Try:
"Sit in a place where you can be successful."	"Sit at another table where you can pay attention to your work."
"We don't have maid service here."	"Clean up your work area."
"I don't want to have to remind you about our math routine."	"Bring your math books."
"It sounds like somebody needs to work harder."	"Casey, it's time to do this assignment right now."
"Do you want me to take those toys away?"	"Put those toys away."
"Be nice."	"Help Evan clean up the paper."

NAMING THE DESIRED BEHAVIOR

Instead of:	Try:
"Stop running!"	"Stop. Walk."
"Lots of you are wasting time."	"We'll begin when you're all seated with your folder on your desk."
"These tables are a mess."	"Clean off your tables before you line up."
"Why are you moving before you've gotten directions?"	"Stop. Wait to hear the directions."
"How many times do I have to say 'No talking right now'?"	"It's time to listen."
"Why aren't you lined up yet?"	"Everyone line up and face forward."

REPLACING QUESTIONS AND SUGGESTIONS WITH STATEMENTS

Instead of:	Try:
"Would you come sit by me?"	"Come sit by me."
"I'm going to ask table one to quiet down."	"Table one, quiet down."
"Will you look at me?"	"Eyes on me."
"Can you put your backpacks away?"	"All backpacks on their hooks."
"Will you please concentrate?"	"It's time to read your book now."
"Will you get ready to work for me?"	"I will begin when everyone has supplies out and is ready to listen for directions."
"I suggest you put those back where they belong."	"Put the game cards away now."

More Examples of Redirecting Language

Group sessions

"Hands down until the speaker has finished talking."

"Stop and think. Then raise your hands if you have an idea."

"It's time to listen now."

"Use quiet voices."

"Tell your feet to hold still."

"Look at the chart."

Independent work sessions

"Scissors are for cutting paper only."

"Take turns with the markers."

"It's time to sit at your table and work now."

"Pick up the paper on the floor."

"Find a place to work where you can concentrate and finish the
    job."

"Use kind words."

"The rulers are for sharing."

Transitions

"Stop. Finish cleanup now."

"When you've pushed your chairs in and lined up, we can go."

"Freeze." Then, "Get your shoes for gym."

"Carry the scissors safely."

"When you have put your books away, we'll begin."

"Walk."

"Help John clean up."

The Process of Developing More Effective Teacher Language

E ffective teacher language is a skill. Developing it, like developing any significant skill, consists of many small steps. Below are the typical stages in this process of changing teacher language, followed by strategies that many teachers have found helpful.

Some teachers progress through these steps faster, others slower; but no one changes radically overnight. Regardless of how quickly you tend to develop new habits, and whether you are just beginning or are well into your journey to improve your teacher language, set reasonable goals and give yourself enough time to meet them before moving on to the next step. Look to this book, other resources, colleagues, and friends for information and support. Over time, through learning and practice, your language will become ever more conducive to children's learning, and ever more powerful in bringing forth your best teaching.

STAGES IN CHANGING TEACHER LANGUAGE

1. WE DECIDE TO MAKE A CHANGE.

As we become more aware of how language affects children, we begin to notice aspects of our own language that we want to continue and aspects we want to change. Perhaps we want to adopt more constructive phrases; perhaps we want to change our tone or pacing. Regardless, it may be best to work on changing only one aspect at a time. For example, we might decide to give more specific feedback such as "You checked over your work carefully before deciding it was done" rather than general praise such as "Good job!"

2. We catch ourselves when we use counterproductive language.

In this stage, we catch ourselves using the language we want to get rid of and silently rehearse more constructive language to try in the future. For example, we're conscious that we said "Good job!" or "Excellent work!" right after we say it, then think to ourselves, "Next time in this situation I could say 'I see you used cursive to write some of the words. That's new for you.'" This is also when we become more aware of the constructive teacher language we are using, noting the ways children respond to it and reminding ourselves to use such language more often.

Before long, we find that we're able to stop ourselves midsentence and reword so that we more accurately communicate the positive message intended. "Nice ... "—we cut ourselves off before saying "job," then add, "You're using cursive to write some of the words." This phase eventually evolves into a more proactive approach in which we catch ourselves before any words escape and we deliberately select the skillful language that best meets our goals.

We're now well on our way to a permanent change, but the new way of speaking may still feel awkward. Over time our use of counterproductive language decreases and our use of productive language increases. We notice how this change is benefiting our interactions with students.

3. We begin to think in new language patterns.

Finally, we start to think in the language that we've worked so hard to cultivate. For example, now when we want to give instructive feedback we almost always immediately think in descriptions of students' specific positive behaviors, such as "I noticed you chose to try some of the hard problems too, rather than just sticking with the easy ones." General praise such as "Good job!" is now naturally reserved for truly celebratory moments with students. Our new language now feels fairly effortless and truly expresses our positive approach to teaching.

STRATEGIES FOR CHANGING
TEACHER LANGUAGE

* Record yourself in the classroom for short periods each day. Play back the recording to hear your words and tone.

* Ask a colleague to sit in your room for fifteen minutes and write down words and phrases you use often.

* Set a reasonable goal. Focus on one aspect of language to change at a time. Give yourself enough time to make the shift.

* When you say a word or phrase you'd rather not say, practice in the moment by replacing the words with something more constructive.

* Take a breath and think before you speak.

* Get a colleague, your grade cluster, or the whole staff to focus on changing the same word or phrase.

* Put replacement words on a card you carry with you or high up on classroom walls as a reminder to yourself.

* Use signals instead of words to get attention. Give yourself space to think more clearly about the appropriate use of words.

* Try to use open-ended questions as a way to interact with students.

About the Author

Paula Denton began teaching children in 1982 and working as a *Responsive Classroom* consulting teacher in 1990. She left the classroom in 1999 to focus full-time on teacher education and later managed program development at Northeast Foundation for Children. Paula has taught courses for pre-service teachers at Antioch New England Graduate School and the University of Massachusetts. She has an EdD degree from the University of Massachusetts. Paula is the author of *Learning Through Academic Choice* and co-author of *The First Six Weeks of School*.

Learn more about
Responsive Classroom® practices

The Morning Meeting Book

By Roxann Kriete with contributions by Lynn Bechtel

For K–8 teachers (2002) 228 pages

Use Morning Meeting in your classroom to build community, increase students' investment in learning, and improve academic and social skills. This book features: ▪ Step-by-step guidelines for holding Morning Meeting ▪ A chapter on Morning Meeting in middle schools ▪ 45 greetings and 66 group activities ▪ Frequently asked questions and answers

The First Six Weeks of School

By Paula Denton and Roxann Kriete

For K–6 teachers (2000) 232 pages

Structure the first weeks of school to lay the groundwork for a productive year of learning. ▪ Guidelines for the first six weeks, including daily plans for the first three weeks for grades K–2, grades 3–4, and grades 5–6 ▪ Ideas for building community, teaching routines, introducing engaging curriculum, fostering autonomy ▪ Games, activities, greetings, songs, read-alouds, and resources especially useful during the early weeks of school

Classroom Spaces That Work

By Marlynn K. Clayton with Mary Beth Forton

For K–6 teachers (2001) 192 pages

Create a physical environment that is welcoming, well suited to the needs of students and teachers, and conducive to social and academic excellence. ▪ Practical ideas for arranging furniture ▪ Suggestions for selecting and organizing materials ▪ Ideas for creating displays ▪ Guidelines for setting up a meeting area ▪ Tips for making the space healthy

RULES IN SCHOOL: TEACHING DISCIPLINE IN THE RESPONSIVE CLASSROOM®, 2ND EDITION

By Kathryn Brady, Mary Beth Forton, and Deborah Porter

For K–8 teachers (2011) 256 pages

Establish a calm, safe learning environment and teach children self-discipline with this approach to classroom rules. ▪ Guidelines for creating rules with students based on their hopes and dreams for school ▪ Steps in modeling and role playing the rules ▪ How to reinforce the rules through language ▪ Using logical consequences when needed

LEARNING THROUGH ACADEMIC CHOICE

By Paula Denton, EdD

For K–6 teachers (2005) 224 pages

Enhance students' learning with this powerful tool for structuring lessons and activities. ▪ Information on building a strong foundation for Academic Choice ▪ Step-by-step look at Academic Choice in action ▪ Practical advice for creating an Academic Choice lesson plan ▪ Many ideas for Academic Choice activities

PARENTS & TEACHERS WORKING TOGETHER

By Carol Davis and Alice Yang

For K–6 teachers (2005) 232 pages

Build school-home cooperation and involve parents in ways that support their children's learning. ▪ Working with diverse family cultures ▪ Building positive relationships in the early weeks of school ▪ Keeping in touch all year long ▪ Involving parents in classroom life, including parents who can't physically come to school ▪ Problem solving with parents

About the *Responsive Classroom*® Approach

This book grew out of the work of Northeast Foundation for Children, Inc. (NEFC) and an approach to teaching known as the *Responsive Classroom* approach. Developed by classroom teachers, this approach consists of highly practical strategies for integrating social and academic learning throughout the school day.

More information and guidance on the Responsive Classroom *approach are available through:*

PUBLICATIONS AND RESOURCES

- Books and videos for elementary school educators
- Website with articles and other information: www.responsiveclassroom.org
- Free quarterly newsletter for elementary educators

PROFESSIONAL DEVELOPMENT OPPORTUNITIES

- One-day and week-long workshops for teachers
- Classroom consultations and other services at individual schools and school districts
- Multifaceted professional development for administrators and all staff at schools wishing to implement the *Responsive Classroom* approach schoolwide

FOR DETAILS, CONTACT:

Northeast Foundation for Children, Inc.
85 Avenue A, Suite 204, P. O. Box 718
Turners Falls, MA 01376-0718

800-360-6332 Fax: 877-206-3952 ■ www.responsiveclassroom.org